AṢṬĀVAKRA SAṀHITĀ

AṢṬĀVAKRA SAṀHITĀ

Text, with word-for-word Translation,
English Rendering, Comments, and Index

SWAMI NITYASWARUPANANDA

Introduction by
Dr. Satkari Mookerjee, M.A., Ph.D.

Advaita Ashrama
(Publication Department)
5 Dehi Entally Road
Kolkata 700 014

Published by
Swami Bodhasarananda
President, Advaita Ashrama
Mayavati, Champawat, Uttarakhand
from its Publication Department, Kolkata
Email: mail@advaitaashrama.org
Website: www.advaitaashrama.org

First Edition, 1940
Fourteenth Impression, September 2008
3M3C

ISBN 81-85301-13-1

Printed in India at
Gipidi Box Co.
Kolkata 700 014

धर्माधमौँ सुखं दुःखं मानसानि न ते विभो ।
न कर्तासि न भोक्तासि मुक्त एवासि सर्वदा ॥६॥

विभो O all-pervading one धर्माधमौँ virtue and
vice सुखं pleasure दुःखं pain मानसानि mental ते yours
न not (त्वम् you) कर्ता doer न not असि are भोक्ता
enjoyer न not असि are सर्वदा ever मुक्तः free एव surely
असि are.

6. Virtue and vice,[1] pleasure and pain,[2] are
of the mind, not of you, O all-pervading one. You
are neither doer nor enjoyer. Verily you are ever
free.

[1] *Virtue and vice*—These spring respectively from
right and wrong actions.
[2] *Pleasure and pain*—effects of virtue and vice on the
mind.
Virtue and vice, pleasure and pain, are all mental
states which affect us only when we identify ourselves
with the mind and think of ourselves as doers and en-
joyers.

एको द्रष्टासि सर्वस्य मुक्तप्रायोऽसि सर्वदा ।
अयमेव हि ते बन्धो द्रष्टारं पश्यसीतरम् ॥७॥

(त्वम् You) सर्वस्य of all एकः one द्रष्टा seer असि are
सर्वदा ever मुक्तप्रायः really free असि are हि surely अयम्
this एव alone ते your बन्धः bondage (यत् that त्वम् you)
द्रष्टारं the seer इतरम् as another पश्यसि see.

7. You are the one seer[1] of all and are really

which is the substratum of the universe, remains eternally pure and unaffected. We are that Consciousness. Therefore we must cease identifying ourselves with the superimposed universe, and thus we shall be happy.

मुक्ताभिमानी मुक्तो हि बद्धो बद्धाभिमान्यपि ।
किंवदन्तीह सत्येयं या मतिः सा गतिर्भवेत् ॥११॥

हि Surely मुक्ताभिमानी one who considers himself free मुक्तः free बद्धाभिमानी one who considers himself bound अपि also बद्धः bound (भवति is) या as मतिः the thought सा so गतिः attainment भवेत् is इह in this world इयं this किंवदन्ती popular saying सत्या true.

11. He[1] who considers himself free is free indeed, and he who considers himself bound remains bound. 'As one thinks, so one becomes' is a popular saying in this world, and it is quite true.

[1] *He etc.*—This is a very significant utterance and one that contains an invaluable lesson for those who wish to attain Self-realization. In reality the Self is ever free, It never enters into a state of bondage. It is our ignorance that we think ourselves bound; and this thought makes our supposed bondage persist and continue. If, however, we constantly think of ourselves as the eternally free Self, we shall realize that we are ever free.

आत्मा साक्षी विभुः पूर्ण एको मुक्तश्चिदक्रियः ।
असङ्गो निस्पृहः शान्तो भ्रमात् संसारवानिव ॥१२॥

CHAPTER IV

GLORIFICATION OF SELF-REALIZATION

जनक उवाच ।

हन्तात्मज्ञस्य धीरस्य खेलतो भोगलीलया ।
न हि संसारवाहीकैर्मूढैः सह समानता ॥ १ ॥

जनक: Janaka उवाच said:

हन्त Oh भोगलीलया with the game of enjoyment खेलत: playing धीरस्य the man of understanding आत्मज्ञस्य of the knower of the Self मूढैः deluded संसार-वाहीकैः beasts of burden of the world सह with समानता similarity न not हि surely (अस्ति is).

Janaka said:

1. Oh, the man of understanding, the knower of the Self, who[1] plays the game of life has no similarity to the deluded beasts[2] of burden of the world.

In this chapter Janaka replies to the charges made by Aṣṭāvakra in the previous chapter. See introductory note on Chapter III, verse 1.

[1] *Who etc.*—Because the joys and sorrows of the world are like play to a man of realization who is unattached to the world and is not affected by it.

[2] *Beasts etc.*—men who, through ignorance, are attached to the world and buffeted by its joys and miseries. They cannot look upon the world as play, or as a juggler's show.

यत्पदं प्रेप्सवो दीनाः शक्राद्याः सर्वदेवताः ।

अहो तत्र स्थितो योगी न हर्षमुपगच्छति ॥ २ ॥

अहो Oh शक्राद्याः beginning with Indra सर्वदेवताः all gods यत्पदं which state प्रेप्सवः hankering after दीनाः unhappy (वर्तन्ते become) तत्र there स्थितः abiding योगी yogin हर्षम् elation न not उपगच्छति attains.

2. Oh, the yogin does[1] not feel elated abiding in that state[2] which Indra and all other gods hanker after and thus become unhappy.[3]

[1] *Does etc.*—Because he feels that he is in his own natural state.

[2] *State*—Existence-Knowledge-Bliss Absolute.

[3] *Unhappy*—Because they cannot attain It.

तज्ज्ञस्य पुण्यपापाभ्यां स्पर्शो ह्यन्तर्न जायते ।

न ह्याकाशस्य धूमेन दृश्यमानापि सङ्गतिः ॥ ३ ॥

तज्ज्ञस्य Of one who has known That अन्तः of inside पुण्यपापाभ्यां (सह) with virtue and vice स्पर्शः touch हि surely न not जायते is हि as आकाशस्य of the sky धूमेन (सह) with smoke सङ्गतिः contact दृश्यमाना appearing अपि though न not (जायते exists).

3. Surely the heart of one who has known the Self is not touched by virtue and vice, just as the sky is not touched by smoke, even though it appears to be.

आत्मैवेदं जगत्सर्वं ज्ञातं येन महात्मना ।

यदृच्छया वर्तमानं तं निषेद्धुं क्षमेत कः ॥ ४ ॥

येन By whom महात्मना the great-souled one इदं this सर्वं all जगत् universe आत्मा Self एव alone (इति this) ज्ञातं is known तं him यदृच्छया according as he likes वर्तमानं remaining क: who निषेद्धं to prohibit क्षमेत can.

4. Who can prevent that great-souled one, who has known this entire universe to be the Self alone, from acting spontaneously?

The idea is : The man of Supreme Realization is beyond all scriptural injunctions. He is quite indifferent to all the prescribed laws of conduct. For these are all formulated for ignorant minds. That, however, does not mean moral anarchy. The man of realization does not stoop to evil actions, as all evil propensities (*saṁskāras*) are annihilated before the highest state of realization is reached. An expert dancer never takes a wrong step.

आब्रह्मस्तम्बपर्यन्ते भूतग्रामे चतुर्विधे ।
विज्ञस्यैव हि सामर्थ्यमिच्छानिच्छाविवर्जने ॥ ५ ॥

आब्रह्मस्तम्बपर्यन्ते From Brahmā down to a clump of grass चतुर्विधे of four kinds भूतग्रामे in all beings विज्ञस्य of the wise one एव alone हि surely इच्छानिच्छाविवर्जने in renouncing desire and aversion सामर्थ्यम् strength (भवति is).

5. Of the four[1] kinds of created beings, from Brahmā down to a clump of grass, it[2] is the wise one alone who is capable of renouncing desire and aversion.

[1] *Four etc.*—namely, *jarāyuja*, born from a womb; *aṇḍaja*, born from an egg; *svedaja*, generated by warm

vapour or sweat; and *udbhijja*, sprouting up. Here it means the entire creation comprising also gods and other subtle beings.

[2] *It etc.*—As long as a man is ignorant of his own true nature and that of the universe, he must have desires and aversions. Certain things he will consider good and desirable, and others the opposite. But one who has known himself and the world as Brahman, sees only One and has therefore no special likes or dislikes. He takes things playfully. He may seem attached to a thing one moment, but the next moment he may totally forget it.

आत्मानमद्वयं कश्चिज्जानाति जगदीश्वरम् ।

यद्वेत्ति तत् स कुरुते न भयं तस्य कुत्रचित् ॥ ६ ॥

कश्चित् Scarcely one आत्मानम् Self अद्वयं non-dual जगदीश्वरम् lord of the universe जानाति knows स: he यत् which वेत्ति knows तत् that कुरुते does तस्य his कुत्रचित् anywhere भयं fear न not (अस्ति is).

6. Rare is the man who knows the Self as One without a second and as lord of the universe. He does[1] what he considers worth doing and has[2] no fear from any quarter.

[1] *Does etc.*—The man of Self-knowledge acts merely under the impulsion of the effects of his actions in the past life *(prārabdha)*. As he is free from the sense of doer, his actions do not produce any binding effects upon his mind. His actions are completely free and spontaneous.

[2] *Has etc.*—Because he sees nothing outside himself.

CHAPTER V

FOUR WAYS TO DISSOLUTION

अष्टावक्र उवाच ।

न ते सङ्गोऽस्ति केनापि किं शुद्धस्त्यक्तुमिच्छसि ।
सङ्घातविलयं कुर्वन्नेवमेव लयं व्रज ॥ १ ॥

अष्टावक्र: Aṣṭāvakra उवाच said:

ते Your केन with anything अपि verily सङ्ग: contact
न not अस्ति is (अत: so) शुद्ध: pure (त्वं you) किं what
त्यक्तुं to renounce इच्छसि wish सङ्घातविलयं dissolution
of the complex कुर्वन् effecting एवम् thus एव surely लयं
the state of dissolution व्रज attain.

Aṣṭāvakra said:

1. You are free from contact with anything
whatsoever. Therefore, pure as you are, what[1] do you
want to renounce? Destroy the body-complex[2] and
in[3] this way enter into the state of dissolution.[4]

In this chapter Aṣṭāvakra describes four different
methods through which *laya*, the state of dissolution, can
be attained. In this absolute state the consciousness of
body, mind, and the senses vanishes.

[1] *What etc.*—We can only renounce or desire what
we are attached to. But the pure Self is unattached.

[2] *Body-complex*—the aggregate of the body, mind,
egoism, and senses. The Self is unattached; through ignorance we identify the Self with the body-complex.
This identification prevents us from realizing the Self.

The moment we destroy this identification, we merge into the Absolute.

[3] *In this way*—by destroying the identification of the Self with body, mind, and the senses.

[4] *Dissolution*—vanishing of the ego and the body and hence merger in Brahman.

उदेति भवतो विश्वं वारिधेरिव बुद्बुदः ।
इति ज्ञात्वैकमात्मानमेवमेव लयं व्रज ॥ २ ॥

वारिधेः From the sea बुद्बुदः bubbles इव like भवतः from you विश्वम् universe उदेति rises इति thus आत्मानम् Self एकं One ज्ञात्वा knowing एवम् in this way एव verily लयं the state of dissolution व्रज attain.

2. The universe rises from you like[1] bubbles rising from the sea. Thus know the Self to be One and in[2] this way enter into the state of dissolution.

[1] *Like etc.*—Water is the only substance of the sea as well as of bubbles, the name and form of the bubbles being only apparent. Similarly, the Self is the only substance behind the universe, the name and form of the universe being mere superimpositions.

[2] *In this way*—having known the oneness of the Self.

प्रत्यक्षमप्यवस्तुत्वाद्विश्वं नास्त्यमले त्वयि ।
रज्जुसर्पं इव व्यक्तमेवमेव लयं व्रज ॥ ३ ॥

रज्जुसर्पं The snake in the rope एव like व्यक्तम् manifested विश्वं universe प्रत्यक्षम् visible अपि though अवस्तुत्वात् on account of being unsubstantial अमले pure त्वयि in you न not अस्ति is एवम् thus एव verily लयं the state of dissolution व्रज attain.

3. The universe, because it is unreal, being manifested[1] like the snake in the rope, does not exist in you who are pure,[2] even though it is present to the senses. Therefore in[3] this way enter into the state of dissolution.

[1] *Manifested etc.*—This classic example of the snake in the rope indicates that the universe which has been superimposed on the Self is really non-existent.

[2] *Pure*—The illusion of the world can never affect the Self.

[3] *In this way*—having known the universe to be non-real and illusory.

समदुःखसुखः पूर्ण आशानैराश्যयोः समः ।
समजीवितमृत्युः सन्नेवमेव लयं व्रज ॥ ४ ॥

पूर्णः Perfect समदुःखसुखः to whom misery and happiness are the same आशानैराश्যयोः in hope and despair सम: same समजीवितमृत्युः to whom life and death are the same सन् being एवम् thus एव verily लयं the state of dissolution व्रज attain.

4. You are perfect and the same in misery and happiness, hope and despair, and life and death. Therefore in[1] this way enter into the state of dissolution.

We are affected by joy and sorrow, hope and despair, life and death as long as we consider ourselves as other than the Self. The moment we know ourselves as the Self which alone exists, we go beyond all pairs of opposites and are unaffected by them, and realize our free nature.

[1] *In this way*—remaining unaffected by the pairs of opposites.

CHAPTER VI

THE HIGHER KNOWLEDGE

जनक उवाच ।

आकाशवदनन्तोऽहं घटवत् प्राकृतं जगत् ।
इति ज्ञानं तथैतस्य न त्यागो न ग्रहो लयः ॥ १ ॥

जनकः Janaka उवाच said:

अहं I आकाशवत् like space अनन्तः limitless प्राकृतं
phenomenal जगत् world घटवत् like a jar इति this ज्ञानं
Knowledge (भवति is) तथा so एतस्य of this त्यागः
relinquishment न not ग्रहः acceptance न not लयः dissolution (न not च and भवति is).

Janaka said:

1. Boundless as space am I, and the phenomenal world is like a jar; this[1] is Knowledge. So[2]
it has neither to be renounced nor accepted nor
destroyed.

As in Chapters III and IV, the dialogue between
Aṣṭāvakra and Janaka in Chapters V and VI is intended
to bring into bold relief the nature of Supreme Knowledge.
In the previous chapter Aṣṭāvakra spoke of *laya*, dissolution, of the need and methods of merging the relative
consciousness into the Absolute. Janaka in reply speaks
here of a higher outlook in which even this attempt at
dissolution arises out of a vestige of ignorance; for the
pure Self was never at any time limited.

[1]*This etc.*—Just as the space inside a jar is the same as the infinite space outside it, so the universe exists in and through the One, infinite Self. The universe has no separate existence of its own. It is a mere illusion. Its existence is only in name and form.

[2] *So*—When Supreme Knowledge has been attained, there is then only the One, infinite Self; the question of renouncing, accepting, or destroying anything does not arise.

महोदधिरिवाहं स प्रपञ्चो वीचिसन्निभः ।
इति ज्ञानं तथैतस्य न त्यागो न ग्रहो लयः ॥ २ ॥

स: That अहं I महोदधि: ocean इव like (अस्मि am) प्रपञ्च: phenomenal universe वीचिसन्निभ: like the wave (भवति is) इति etc. *as before.*

2. I am like[1] the ocean and the universe is like the wave; this is Knowledge. So it has neither to be renounced nor accepted nor destroyed.

[1] *Like etc.*—This example makes clearer the oneness of the Self. Water is the real substance; the name and form of the wave are only apparent. Similarly, the Self is the only substance; the name and form of the universe are only illusory superimpositions.

अहं स शुक्तिसङ्काशो रूप्यवद्विश्वकल्पना ।
इति ज्ञानं तथैतस्य न त्यागो न ग्रहो लयः ॥ ३ ॥

स: That अहं I शुक्तिसङ्काश: like mother of pearl (अस्मि am) विश्वकल्पना the illusion of the universe रूप्यवत् like silver (भवति is) इति etc. *as before.*

3. I am like mother of pearl and the illusion of the universe is like[1] silver; this is Knowledge. So

it has neither to be renounced nor accepted nor
destroyed.

¹ *Like etc.*—The reality behind the illusion of silver
is the mother of pearl. In the same way the reality behind
the universe is the Self itself.

अहं वा सर्वभूतेषु सर्वभूतान्यथो मयि ।

इति ज्ञानं तथैतस्य न त्यागो न ग्रहो लयः ॥ ४ ॥

अहं I वा indeed सर्वभूतेषु in all beings (अस्मि am)
अथो and सर्वभूतानि all beings मयि in me (सन्ति are)
इति etc. *as before.*

4. I¹ am indeed in all beings, and all² beings
are in me. This is Knowledge. So it has neither to
be renounced nor accepted nor destroyed.

¹ *I etc.*—The Self is the only substance of the universe.

² *All etc.*—The Self is the substratum, the One Existence, on which the universe is a mere superimposition.

CHAPTER VII

NATURE OF SELF-REALIZATION

जनक उवाच ।

मय्यनन्तमहाम्भोधौ विश्वपोत इतस्ततः ।
भ्रमति स्वान्तवातेन न ममास्त्यसहिष्णुता ॥ १ ॥

जनकः Janaka उवाच said:

अनन्तमहाम्भोधौ In the boundless ocean मयि in me विश्वपोतः the ark of the universe स्वान्तवातेन by the wind of its own nature इतस्ततः hither and thither भ्रमति moves मम my असहिष्णुता impatience न not अस्ति is.

Janaka said:

1. In me, the boundless ocean, the ark of the universe moves hither and thither impelled by the wind of its own inherent nature. I am not impatient.[1]

[1] *Impatient*—affected.

When the wind rises on the ocean, it tosses a ship hither and thither and even, through its impact, sends it down. But the ocean is not affected by the movements of the ship. Similarly, the universe, which rests on the reality of the Self, is ever changing under the impulsion of its inherent laws. But the changing world does not affect the Self in the least.

मय्यनन्तमहाम्भोधौ जगद्वीचिः स्वभावतः ।
उदेतु वास्तमायातु न मे वृद्धिर्न च क्षतिः ॥ २ ॥

अनन्तमहाम्भोधौ In the limitless ocean मयि in me जगद्वीचि: the wave of the world स्वभावत: by its own nature उदेतु may rise अस्तम् dissolution आयातु may attain वा or मे my वृद्धि: increase न not क्षति: decrease न not च and (भवति is).

2. In me, the limitless ocean, let the wave of the world rise or vanish of itself. I neither increase nor decrease thereby.

A wave is no other than the water of the ocean itself; only name and form have been added; there is no increase in substance. Exactly so is the world; its reality is the Self itself. So when the world appears, name and form are superimposed on the reality of the Self; and when it disappears, name and form vanish. The reality is ever the same.

मय्यनन्तमहाम्भोधौ विश्वं नाम विकल्पना ।
अतिशान्तो निराकार एतदेवाहमास्थितः ॥ ३ ॥

अनन्तमहाम्भोधौ In the boundless ocean मयि in me विश्वं universe नाम called विकल्पना imagination (अस्ति is अहम् I) अतिशान्त: highly tranquil निराकार: formless (अस्मि am) एतत् this एव alone अहम् I आस्थित: abide in.

3. In me, the boundless ocean, is the imagination of the universe. I am quite tranquil and formless. In this[1] alone do I abide.

[1] *This*—namely, the Knowledge that the world is merely an appearance and that the Self in which it appears remains ever calm and formless.

नात्मा भावेषु नो भावस्तत्रानन्ते निरञ्जने ।
इत्यसक्तोऽस्पृहः शान्त एतदेवाहमास्थितः ॥ ४ ॥

आत्मा Self भावेषु in the objects न not (अस्ति is)
भावः object अनन्ते limitless निरञ्जने stainless तत्र in that
(Self) नो not (अस्ति is) इति so (आत्मा Self) असक्तः
unattached अस्पृहः desireless शान्तः tranquil (अस्ति is)
एतत् this एव alone अहम् I आस्थितः abide in.

4. The Self[1] is not in the object, nor[2] is the
object in the Self which is infinite and stainless.
Thus It is free from attachment and desire, and
tranquil. In this alone do I abide.

[1] *Self etc.*—The Self is all-pervasive and infinite. It
cannot therefore be contained by finite objects, such as
body and mind.

[2] *Nor etc.*—Because all objects are superimposed on
the Self and therefore do not really exist in the Self.

अहो चिन्मात्रमेवाहमिन्द्रजालोपमं जगत् ।
अतो मम कथं कुत्र हेयोपादेयकल्पना ॥ ५ ॥

अहो Oh अहम् I चिन्मात्रम् Consciousness itself एव
surely जगत् world इन्द्रजालोपमं like a magic show अतः
so मम my कुत्र where कथं how हेयोपादेयकल्पना thought of
the rejectable and the acceptable (स्यात् can be).

5. Oh, I am really Consciousness itself. The
world is like a juggler's show. So how and where
can there be any thought of rejection and acceptance in me?

A man of Self-realization looks upon this world as a juggler's show, false and illusory, and having no existence even though it is visible to him. Therefore no object whatsoever in the world can either attract or repel him.

CHAPTER VIII

BONDAGE AND LIBERATION

अष्टावक्र उवाच ।

तदा बन्धो यदा चित्तं किञ्चिद्वाञ्छति शोचति ।
किञ्चिन्मुञ्चति गृह्णाति किञ्चिद्धृष्यति कुप्यति ॥ १ ॥

अष्टावक्र: Aṣṭāvakra उवाच said:

यदा When चित्तं mind किञ्चित् anything वाञ्छति desires शोचति grieves किञ्चित् anything मुञ्चति rejects गृह्णाति accepts किञ्चित् anything हृष्यति feels joy for कुप्यति feels angry for तदा then बन्ध: bondage (अस्ति is).

Aṣṭāvakra said:

1. It is bondage when the mind desires or grieves at anything, rejects or accepts anything, feels happy or angry at anything.

तदा मुक्तिर्यदा चित्तं न वाञ्छति न शोचति ।
न मुञ्चति न गृह्णाति न हृष्यति न कुप्यति ॥ २ ॥

यदा When चित्तं mind न not वाञ्छति desires न not शोचति grieves न not मुञ्चति rejects न not गृह्णाति accepts न not हृष्यति feels joy न not कुप्यति is angry तदा then मुक्ति: freedom.

2. Liberation is attained when the mind does not desire or grieve or reject or accept or feel happy or angry.

6

Desiring, grieving, etc., are the modifications of the *chitta*, the mind-stuff, which may be likened respectively to a lake and its ripples. The depths of the lake are, as it were, our own true Self. We can only catch a glimpse of the depths when the water is calm and clear and there are no waves. If the water is muddy or agitated, the depths will not be seen. Likewise, as long as there are mental modifications, which are possible only so long as we identify ourselves with them, we cannot see the Self and are in ignorance and bondage. But when the mind is calm and free from such modifications, we realize our true nature and thus attain liberation.

तदा बन्धो यदा चित्तं सक्तं कास्वपि दृष्टिषु ।
तदा मोक्षो यदा चित्तमसक्तं सर्वदृष्टिषु ॥ ३ ॥

यदा When चित्त mind कासु अपि to any दृष्टिषु sense experiences सक्तं attached तदा then बन्ध: bondage यदा when चित्तम् mind सर्वदृष्टिषु in all sense experiences असक्तं unattached तदा then मोक्ष: liberation.

3. It is bondage when the mind is attached to any sense experience.[1] It is liberation when the mind is detached from all sense experiences.

In the two preceding verses, bondage and freedom have been explained as identification with and dissociation from the *internal*, mental, modifications. Here they are explained in reference to *external* objects.

[1] *Sense experience—Dṛṣṭi* means seeing, and hence any sense experience.

यदा नाहं तदा मोक्षो यदाहं बन्धनं तदा ।
मत्वेति हेलया किञ्चित् मा गृहाण विमुञ्च मा ॥ ४ ॥

यदा When अहं I न not तदा then मोक्ष: liberation

यदा when अहं I तदा then बन्धनं bondage इति thus
मत्वा thinking हेलया easily किञ्चित् anything मा not गृहाण
accept मा not विमुञ्च reject (वा or).

4. When there is no 'I', there is liberation;
when there is 'I', there is bondage. Considering
thus, easily refrain from accepting or rejecting anything.

Egoism is bondage, constituting as it does the identification of the Self with body and mind; and ego-lessness
is liberation. When there is no ego, there is no identification of the Self with body and mind, and the Self
is realized as One without a second, pervading the whole
universe. Having this knowledge one becomes perfectly
tranquil and free from desire or aversion.

CHAPTER IX

DETACHMENT

अष्टावक्र उवाच ।

कृताकृते च द्वन्द्वानि कदा शान्तानि कस्य वा ।
एवं ज्ञात्वेह निर्वेदाद्भव त्यागपरोऽव्रती ॥ १ ॥

अष्टावक्र: Aṣṭāvakra उवाच said:

कृताकृते Duties done and not done द्वन्द्वानि pairs of opposites च and कदा when कस्य whose वा or शान्तानि ended एवं thus ज्ञात्वा knowing इह in this world निर्वेदात् through indifference त्यागपर: intent on renunciation अव्रती desireless भव be.

Aṣṭāvakra said:

1. Duties done and not done, as well as the pairs of opposites—when[1] do they cease and for whom? Knowing thus, be desireless[2] and intent on renunciation through complete indifference to the world.

[1] *When etc.*—Our life is a mixture of opposites like joy and sorrow, success and failure, and good and evil. And we always have preferences which cause us to choose certain things to be done and others avoided. Hence our conception of duty. As long as we consider this world to be real, we cannot escape the pairs of opposites nor eradicate the sense of duty. The only way out of this state of things is to realize the unreality of the world, and renounce our identification with it.

² *Desireless*—Literally, one not performing a religious rite or observing a vow. These rites and vows presuppose a desire for earthly or heavenly prosperity.

कस्यापि तात धन्यस्य लोकचेष्टावलोकनात् ।
जीवितेच्छा बुभुक्षा च बुभुत्सोपशमं गताः ॥ २ ॥

तात Child कस्य whose अपि even धन्यस्य of the blessed one लोकचेष्टावलोकनात् by observing the ways of men जीवितेच्छा desire to live बुभुक्षा desire to enjoy बुभुत्सा desire to know च and उपशमं cessation गताः attained.

2. Rare indeed, my child, is that blessed person whose desire for life, enjoyment, and learning have been extinguished by observing[1] the ways of men.

¹ *Observing etc.*—Some people learn the hollowness of the world by observation. That is to say, by observing the sufferings of others they realize that the world cannot give eternal happiness. But such people are very rare and the majority get this lesson only after plunging into the world and experiencing for themselves the ills of life.

अनित्यं सर्वमेवेदं तापत्रितयदूषितम् ।
असारं निन्दितं हेयमिति निश्चित्य शाम्यति ॥ ३ ॥

इदं This सर्वमेव all verily अनित्यं transient तापत्रितय-दूषितम् vitiated by threefold misery असारं unsubstantial निन्दितं contemptible हेयम् rejectable इति this निश्चित्य knowing for certain (ज्ञानी a wise man) शाम्यति becomes calm.

3. The wise man becomes calm by realizing that all verily is vitiated by the threefold[1] misery

and is transient, unsubstantial, and contemptible, and should be rejected.

¹ *Threefold etc.*—viz. misery pertaining to mind and body, misery caused by animate and inanimate objects, and misery caused by floods, earthquakes, etc.

कोऽसौ कालो वयः किं वा यत्र द्वन्द्वानि नो नृणाम् ।
तान्युपेक्ष्य यथाप्राप्तवर्ती सिद्धिमवाप्नु यात् ॥ ४ ॥

यत्र Where नृणाम् of men द्वन्द्वानि pairs of opposites नो not (सन्ति are) असौ that कालः time कः what वयः age वा or किं what तानि those उपेक्ष्य quitting यथाप्राप्तवर्ती one who rests content with what comes of itself सिद्धिम् perfection अवाप्नु यात् attains.

4. What is that time or that age in which the pairs of opposites do not exist for men? One who, quitting those, is content with what comes of itself attains perfection.

For man no time or age is possible in which there will be unalloyed good and joy, unattended by evil and sorrow. He cannot, therefore, hope to gain joy and peace in the course of life's process. He has to realize the supreme fact that peace and perfection can only be attained by transcending the process of relative life and remaining unattached to its experiences.

नाना मतं महर्षीणां साधूनां योगिनां तथा ।
दृष्ट्वा निर्वेदमापन्नः को न शाम्यति मानवः ॥ ५ ॥

महर्षीणां Of great seers साधूनां of saints तथा as well as योगिनां of yogins मतं opinion नाना diverse दृष्ट्वा seeing

निर्वेदम् indifference आपन्न: attained (सन् being) क: what
मानव: man न not शाम्यति attains peace.

5. What man is there who, having observed
the diversity[1] of opinions among the great seers,
saints, and *yogins*, and become completely indifferent to learning, does not attain quietude?[2]

[1] *Diversity etc.*—refers to the different schools of
philosophy, the *summum bonum* of life being different in
the different schools.

[2] *Quietude*—Those who have attained complete indifference to worldly objects and are solely intent on
Self-realization are sure to be endowed with this rare
quality of mind.

कृत्वा मूर्तिपरिज्ञानं चैतन्यस्य न किं गुरुः ।
निर्वेदसमतायुक्त्या यस्तारयति संसृतेः ॥ ६ ॥

य: Who निर्वेदसमतायुक्त्या by indifference, sameness,
and reasoning चैतन्यस्य of Pure Consciousness मूर्तिपरिज्ञानं
realization of the true nature कृत्वा gaining संसृतेः from
metempsychosis तारयति saves himself स: he किं (interrogative) गुरु: spiritual guide न not.

6. He who gains knowledge of the true nature
of Pure Consciousness by complete indifference to
the world, by equanimity,[1] and by reasoning, and
saves himself from the round of birth and rebirth,
is he[2] not really the spiritual guide?

[1] *Equanimity*—in friendship and enmity, happiness
and misery, and the like.

[2] *He etc.*—The previous verse disqualifies *ṛṣis*,
sādhus, and *yogins* as spiritual guides because of their

varied opinions. The present verse shows that that man alone who has realized the Truth himself can be a spiritual guide. Not merely learned opinions, but actual practice and realization are the *sine qua non* of a Guru.

पश्य भूतविकारांस्त्वं भूतमात्रान् यथार्थतः ।
तत्क्षणाद्बन्धनिर्मुक्तः स्वरूपस्थो भविष्यसि ॥ ७ ॥

भूतविकारान् The modifications of the elements यथार्थतः in reality भूतमात्रान् nothing but the primary elements पश्य see (एवं सति thus) तत्क्षणात् at once त्वं you बन्धनिर्मुक्तः free from bondage (सन् being) स्वरूपस्थः abiding in your own nature भविष्यसि will be.

7. Look upon the modifications[1] of the elements as nothing in reality but the primary elements themselves and you will at once be free[2] from bondage and abide in your true self.

[1] *Modifications etc.*—viz. the body, mind, senses, etc. In reality all these are nothing but the basic elements, differing only in the patterns of combination. It is these patterns of combination that make us consider one thing beautiful and another ugly, and thus desire the one and dislike the other. But the moment we feel all things to be the same, all likes and dislikes will vanish, and we shall know our true nature and be free.

[2] *Free etc.*—Bondage consists in attraction to the body and the things of the world; freedom lies in forgoing that attraction and abiding in the true nature of the Self.

वासना एव संसार इति सर्वा विमुञ्च ताः ।
तत्त्यागो वासनात्यागात् स्थितिरद्य यथा तथा ॥ ८ ॥

वासनाः Desires एव surely संसारः world इति so ताः

those सर्वाः all विमुञ्च renounce वासनात्यागात् from the renunciation of desires तत्त्याग: renunciation of that (भवति is) अद्य now स्थिति: you may live यथा तथा wherever it may be.

8. Desires[1] alone are the world. Do you, therefore, renounce them all. The renunciation of desire is the renunciation of the world. Now[2] you may live anywhere.

[1] *Desires etc.*—Because it is desire that binds us to the world and makes us think it real, and thus subjects us to the round of births and rebirths. The moment we are free from desire, the reality of the world will vanish and there will be no further reincarnation for us.

[2] *Now etc.*—One who has renounced desire is completely free. He may live anywhere for he will not be affected by circumstances.

CHAPTER X

QUIETUDE

अष्टावक्र उवाच ।

विहाय वैरिणं काममर्थं चानर्थसङ्कुलम् ।
धर्ममप्येतयोर्हेतुं सर्वत्रानादरं कुरु ॥ १ ॥

अष्टावक्र: Aṣṭāvakra उवाच said:

वैरिणं Enemy कामम् desire अनर्थसङ्कुलम् full of mischief अर्थ worldly prosperity च and एतयो: of these two हेतुं cause धर्मम् good work अपि also विहाय forsaking सर्वत्र everywhere अनादरं disregard कुरु do.

Aṣṭāvakra said:

1. Cultivate indifference to everything, having given up *kāma* (desire) which is the enemy,[1] *artha* (worldly prosperity) which[2] is attended with mischief, and *dharma*[3] (performance of good works) which is the cause of these two.

[1] *Enemy*—Because desire for sensual enjoyment obstructs the attainment of Knowledge and binds us to the world.

[2] *Which etc.*—Because the acquisition and preservation of wealth lead to habits of mind which are harmful to our higher nature.

[3] *Dharma etc.*—*Dharma* here means good works, both secular and religious. By performing good works we earn merit which confers on us worldly prosperity as well as sensual enjoyment.

Dharma, artha, and *kāma* are the three aims of the ordinary man's existence. But in order to attain *mokṣa,* liberation, which is the *summum bonum* of life, one has to renounce these three aims. The Absolute can never be reached as long as there is the least speck of desire. And without desire all these three aims are meaningless. Hence the necessity of renouncing them, so that our eyes may be opened to the Supreme Self.

स्वप्नेन्द्रजालवत् पश्य दिनानि त्रीणि पञ्च वा ।
मित्रक्षेत्रधनागारदारदायादिसम्पदः ॥ २ ॥

त्रीणि Three पञ्च five वा or दिनानि days (स्थायिन्यः lasting) मित्रक्षेत्रधनागारदारदायादिसम्पदः friends, lands, wealth, houses, wives, presents, and other such good fortunes स्वप्नेन्द्रजालवत् like a dream or a juggler's show पश्य see.

2. Look upon friends, lands, wealth, houses, wives, presents, and other such marks of good fortune, as[1] a dream or a juggler's show, lasting only a few days.

[1] *As etc.*—unreal and transitory.

यत्र यत्र भवेत्तृष्णा संसारं विद्धि तत्र वै ।
प्रौढवैराग्यमाश्रित्य वीततृष्णः सुखी भव ॥ ३ ॥

यत्र यत्र Wherever तृष्णा desire भवेत् is तत्र there वै indeed संसारं world विद्धि know (अतः so) प्रौढवैराग्यम् firm non-attachment आश्रित्य adopting वीततृष्णः free from desire सुखी happy भव be.

3. Know that wherever[1] there is desire there is

the world. Betaking yourself to firm[2] non-attachment, go beyond desire and be happy.

[1] *Wherever etc.*—Because desire for sensual enjoyment
leads man to various actions and binds him to the world
for the enjoyment of their fruits.

[2] *Firm*—indicates an attitude of absolute non-
attachment to the objects of enjoyment.

तृष्णामात्रात्मको बन्धस्तन्नाशो मोक्ष उच्यते ।
भवासंसक्तिमात्रेण प्राप्तितुष्टिर्मुहुर्मुहुः ॥ ४ ॥

बन्ध: Bondage तृष्णामात्रात्मक: consisting in desire
alone तन्नाश: destruction of that मोक्ष: liberation उच्यते is
called भवासंसक्तिमात्रेण by non-attachment to the world
alone मुहुर्मुहुः constantly प्राप्तितुष्टि: joy from attainment
(भवति is).

4. Bondage consists only in desire, and the
destruction of desire is said to be liberation. Only
by non-attachment to the world does one attain
the constant joy of the realization of the Self.

त्वमेकश्चेतन: शुद्धो जडं विश्वमसत्तथा ।
अविद्यापि न किञ्चित्सा का बुभुत्सा तथापि ते ॥ ५ ॥

त्वम् You एक: One शुद्ध: Pure चेतन: Intelligence (असि
are) विश्वम् universe जडं devoid of intelligence तथा and
असत् non-existent (अस्ति is) अविद्या ignorance अपि also
न not किञ्चित् anything (भवति is) तथा अपि yet ते your
का what सा that बुभुत्सा desire to know.

5. You are One, Pure Intelligence. The uni-

verse is non-intelligent[1] and unreal. Ignorance also is no real entity. What can you yet desire to know?

That even the desire to know has to be renounced is emphasized here. We should not desire to know that which is not real. It is the Self alone which is real, and we should know that to be our true nature, while the apparent world and the ignorance that causes us to accept it as real are not really existent. There is therefore nothing else to know but the Self. Hence, even the desire to know has to be renounced.

[1] *Non-intelligent*—The conscious principle in nature is the reflection of the Self. All consciousness is consciousness of the Self; all non-self is thus non-intelligent.

राज्यं सुताः कलत्राणि शरीराणि सुखानि च ।
संसक्तस्यापि नष्टानि तव जन्मनि जन्मनि ॥ ६ ॥

संसक्तस्य Attached अपि though तव your राज्यं kingdom सुताः sons कलत्राणि wives शरीराणि bodies सुखानि pleasures च and जन्मनि जन्मनि birth after birth नष्टानि have been lost.

6. Kingdoms, sons, wives, bodies, and pleasures have been lost to you birth after birth, even though you were attached to them.

This verse gives a common-sense reason why we should have recourse to renunciation. Such is the transitory nature of worldly things that even when we love them dearly, we cannot retain them for long. We lose them and thus they cause us suffering. This process has been repeated life after life. What, then, is the use of being attached to such things?

अलमर्थेन कामेन सुकृतेनापि कर्मणा ।
एभ्यः संसारकान्तारे न विश्रान्तमभून्मनः ॥ ७ ॥

अर्थेन With prosperity कामेन with desire सुकृतेन कर्मणा with pious deed अपि and अलम् no need संसारकान्तारे in the dreary forest of the world मन: mind एभ्य: from these विश्रान्तम् reposed न not अभूत् was.

7. Enough of prosperity, desires, and pious deeds. The mind did not find repose in these in the dreary forest of the world.

Aṣṭāvakra again maintains the worthlessness of *dharma, artha,* and *kāma* as ideals, and emphasizes *mokṣa.* See verse 1 of this chapter.

कृतं न कति जन्मानि कायेन मनसा गिरा ।
दुःखमायासदं कर्म तद्द्याप्युपरम्यताम् ॥ ८ ॥

(त्वं You) कायेन with body मनसा with mind गिरा with speech दुःखम् painful आयासदं involving difficulty कर्म work कति how many जन्मानि births न not कृतं did तत् so अद्य today अपि even उपरम्यताम् cease.

8. For how many births have you not done hard and painful work with body, with mind, and with speech! Therefore cease at least today.

We have our present bodies and experiences as a result of our actions in past incarnations. This process will continue so long as we continue to act in ignorance, and we shall go from birth to birth. To escape misery for ever, we must cease from worldly activity.

Aṣṭāvakra indicates that our past actions, entailing so much labour and suffering, have not given us any lasting happiness. Why should we then continue these worldly actions which spring from ignorance and cause bondage and misery?

CHAPTER XI

WISDOM

अष्टावक्र उवाच ।

भावाभावविकारश्च स्वभावादिति निश्चयी ।
निर्विकारो गतक्लेशः सुखेनैवोपशाम्यति ॥ १ ॥

अष्टावक्र: Aṣṭāvakra उवाच said:

भावाभावविकार: Change in the form of existence and destruction च (expletive) स्वभावात् from nature (जायते comes about) इति this निश्चयी one who has known for certain निर्विकार: unperturbed गतक्लेश: free from pain (सन् being) सुखेन easily एव (expletive) उपशाम्यति finds rest.

Aṣṭāvakra said:

1. He who has realized that change[1] in the form of existence and destruction is in the nature of things, easily[2] finds repose, being unperturbed and free from pain.

[1] *Change etc.*—Everything exists, changes, and is destroyed. This is the nature of everything. Nothing is permanent.

[2] *Easily etc.*—If one realizes the evanescent nature of things, one is no longer attached to them, and thus finds peace. Mental disturbance and pain are caused by our attachment to transitory objects, taking them to be permanent.

ईश्वरः सर्वनिर्माता नेहान्य इति निश्चयी ।
अन्तर्गलितसर्वाशः शान्तः क्वापि न सज्जते ॥ २ ॥

ईश्वरः Iśvara सर्वनिर्माता creator of all इह here अन्यः
other न not (अस्ति is) इति this निश्चयी one who has
known for certain अन्तर्गलितसर्वाशः with all desires gone
from within शान्तः calm (सन् being) क्व अपि in anything
whatsoever न not सज्जते is attached.

2. He who has known for certain that Iśvara[1]
is the creator of all and that there is none else here,[2]
becomes peaceful[3] with all his inner desires set at
rest, and is not attached to anything whatsoever.

[1] *Iśvara etc.*—The universe has arisen from the Self,
exists in the Self, and dissolves in the Self. Whatever
exists in the universe is pervaded by the Self. There is
no existence other than the Self itself.

[2] *Here*—in the universe.

[3] *Peaceful etc.*—Desires arise from thinking that there
are other things and existences outside oneself. One
covets them and wants to enjoy them. But when one
knows that the universe is pervaded by the Self—that
there is only the Self and nothing else—the feeling of
otherness goes and there is no desire, and hence there is
peace.

आपदः सम्पदः काले दैवादेवेति निश्चयी ।
तृप्तः स्वस्थेन्द्रियो नित्यं न वाञ्छति न शोचति ॥ ३ ॥

काले In time आपदः adversities सम्पदः prosperities
दैवात् through the effects of past actions एव certainly
(भवन्ति come) इति this निश्चयी one who has known for
certain नित्यं ever तृप्तः contented स्वस्थेन्द्रियः with all the

senses controlled (सन् being) न not वाञ्छति desires न not शोचति grieves (च and).

3. He who has known for certain that adversity and prosperity come in their own time through the effects[1] of past actions is ever contented, has all his senses under[2] control, and neither desires[3] nor grieves.[4]

[1] *Effects etc.*—Whoever realizes that his present life, with all its vicissitudes, is the result of his past actions, is not affected by the changes of fortune.

[2] *Under etc.*—Unattached to worldly objects.

[3] *Desires*—for what is not attained.

[4] *Grieves*—for what is lost.

सुखदुःखे जन्ममृत्यू दैवादेवेति निश्चयी ।
साध्यादर्शी निरायासः कुर्वन्नपि न लिप्यते ॥ ४ ॥

सुखदुःखे Happiness and misery जन्ममृत्यू birth and death दैवात् due to the effects of past actions एव certainly (भवन्ति are) इति this निश्चयी one who has known for certain साध्यादर्शी not finding anything to accomplish निरायासः free from care (सन् being) कुर्वन् doing अपि even न not लिप्यते is attached.

4. He who knows for certain that happiness and misery, birth and death are due to the effects of past actions, does not find anything to accomplish, and thus becomes free from care and is not[1] attached even though engaged in action.

[1] *Not etc.*—Because he knows that he is not the doer of his actions.

चिन्तया जायते दुःखं नान्यथेहेति निश्चयी ।
तया हीनः सुखी शान्तः सर्वत्र गलितस्पृहः ॥ ५ ॥

इह Here दुःखं misery चिन्तया through care जायते is
produced न not अन्यथा otherwise इति this निश्चयी one
who has known for certain तया हीनः devoid of that
सुखी happy शान्तः peaceful सर्वत्र everywhere गलितस्पृहः
rid of desires (भवति is).

5. He who has realized that it is care[1] and
nothing else that breeds misery in this world, becomes free from it, and is happy, peaceful, and
everywhere rid of desires.

[1] *Care etc.*—Care presupposes identification of the
mind with some worldly object. This again breeds attachment and desire which create bondage and cause suffering.

नाहं देहो न मे देहो बोधोऽहमिति निश्चयी ।
कैवल्यमिव संप्राप्तो न स्मरत्यकृतं कृतम् ॥ ६ ॥

अहं I देहः body न not मे my देहः body न not अहम् I
बोधः Consciousness इति this निश्चयी one who has realized
कैवल्यं the state of Absoluteness संप्राप्तः attained इव as
if अकृतं what is not done कृतम् what is done न not स्मरति
remembers.

6. 'I am not the body nor is the body mine. I
am Consciousness itself '—he who has realized this
for certain does[1] not remember what he has done or
not done as[2] if he has attained the state of Absoluteness.

[1] *Does etc.*—Work pertains to body and mind alone

and not to the Self. He who has attained Supreme Knowledge does not identify himself with body and mind. Therefore he has no connection with any work. He does not think of what he has done and not done, as ordinary people do.

[2] *As etc.*—Because Self-realization, once attained, continues even after the destruction of the body.

आब्रह्मस्तम्बपर्यन्तमहमेवेति निश्चयी ।
निर्विकल्पः शुचिः शान्तः प्राप्ताप्राप्तविनिवृतः ॥ ७ ॥

आब्रह्मस्तम्बपर्यन्तम् From Brahmā down to a clump of grass अहम् I एव verily (अस्मि am) इति this निश्चयी one who knows for certain निर्विकल्पः free from conflict of thought शुचिः pure शान्तः peaceful प्राप्ताप्राप्तविनिवृतः turned away from what is attained and not attained (भवति is).

7. ' I am indeed in everything, from Brahmā down to a clump of grass '—he who knows this for certain becomes free[1] from conflict of thought, pure and peaceful, and free[2] from care for what is attained and not attained.

[1] *Free etc.*—Because mental determination or indetermination is impossible for him who is the cosmic existence itself. He has nothing to determine.

[2] *Free etc.*—Because he does not see anything outside himself.

नानाश्चर्यमिदं विश्वं न किञ्चिदिति निश्चयी ।
निर्वासनः स्फूर्तिमात्रो न किञ्चिदिव शाम्यति ॥ ८ ॥

इदं This नाना manifold आश्चर्यम् wonderful विश्वं universe न not किञ्चित् anything इति this निश्चयी one who

knows for certain निर्वासनः free from desire स्फूर्तिमात्रः
pure Consciousness (सन् being) किञ्चित् anything न
not (अस्ति exists) इव as if शाम्यति finds peace.

8. He who knows for certain that this manifold and wonderful universe is nothing,[1] becomes
desireless and Pure Consciousness, and finds peace
as[2] if nothing exists.

[1] *Nothing*—unreal.

[2] *As etc.*—Though, while living in the body, he may
perceive the apparent existence of the universe, yet his
inner peace is that of the absolute state in which nothing
but the Self exists.

CHAPTER XII

ABIDING IN THE SELF

जनक उवाच ।

कायकृत्यासहः पूर्वं ततो वाग्विस्तरासहः ।
अथ चिन्तासहस्तस्मादेवमेवाहमास्थितः ॥ १ ॥

जनकः Janaka उवाच said:

(अहं I) पूर्वं at first कायकृत्यासहः intolerant of physical action ततः then वाग्विस्तरासहः intolerant of extensive speech अथ then चिन्तासहः intolerant of thought (अभवम् became) तस्मात् so अहम् I एवम् thus एव verily आस्थित abide.

Janaka said:

1. I became intolerant[1] first of physical[2] action, then of extensive speech, and then of thought. Thus[3] therefore do I firmly abide.

In the eight verses of this chapter the disciple describes his state of highest realization.

[1] *Intolerant*—that is to say, detached, the mind having completely turned away from deed, word, and thought, all of which belong to the relative plane.

[2] *Physical etc.*—Discipline was started with the gross, then the subtler obstructions were controlled.

[3] *Thus*—devoid of any action, physical, vocal, or mental.

प्रीत्यभावेन शब्दादेरदृश्यत्वेन चात्मनः ।
विक्षेपैकाग्रहृदय एवमेवाहमास्थितः ॥ २ ॥

शब्दादेः Of sound etc. प्रीत्यभावेन for want of attachment आत्मनः of Self अदृश्यत्वेन being no object of perception च and विक्षेपैकाग्रहृदयः with the mind freed from
distraction and one-pointed अहम् I एवम् thus एव verily
आस्थितः abide.

2. Having no attachment for sound[1] and other
sense objects, and the Self[2] not being an object of
perception, my mind is freed[3] from distraction and
is one-pointed. Thus[4] therefore do I firmly abide.

[1] *Sound etc.*—all perceivable objects, all things of
the universe.

[2] *Self etc.*—Perception is possible only in a state of
duality. The Self is absolute. There cannot be a knower
of it. Hence it cannot be an object of perception.

'When there is duality, as it were, then one smells
something, one sees something, one hears something, one
speaks something, one thinks something, one knows something. (But) when to the knower of Brahman everything
has become the Self, then what should one smell and
through what? What should one see and through what?
What should one hear and through what? What should
one speak and through what? What should one think and
through what? What should one know and through what?
Through what should one know that owing to which
all this is known—through what, O Maitreyi, should one
know the knower?' (*Bṛhadāraṇyaka Upaniṣad*—IV. v. 15)

[3] *Freed etc.*—Attachment to the objects of the senses
distracts the mind and prevents it from being turned
towards the Self. The wise man has no attachment to
the objects of the senses, and as the eternal Self is not

an object of perception, being beyond mind and speech, he is free from all distractions.

4 *Thus*—as the absolute self, beyond all distractions and relativities.

समाध्यासादिविक्षिप्तौ व्यवहार: समाधये ।
एवं विलोक्य नियममेवमेवाहमास्थित: ॥ ३ ॥

समाध्यासादिविक्षिप्तौ In distraction caused by superimposition etc. समाधये for concentration व्यवहार: activity (भवति is) एवं thus नियमम् rule विलोक्य seeing अहम् I एवम् thus एव verily आस्थित: abide.

3. An effort has to be made for concentration when there is distraction of mind owing[1] to superimposition etc. Seeing[2] this to be the rule, thus[3] do I firmly abide.

[1] *Owing etc.*—as in the case of the ignorant man. The ideas of body, mind, egoism, etc. are superimposed on his mind. His mind is distracted, and an effort is required to concentrate it.

[2] *Seeing etc.*—The rule prescribing concentration applies only to a person in a state of ignorance and is meaningless to one who is established in the Self.

[3] *Thus*—beyond concentration.

हेयोपादेयविरहादेवं हर्षविषादयो: ।
अभावाद्य हे ब्रह्मन्नेवमेवाहमास्थित: ॥ ४ ॥

हे O ब्रह्मन् Brahman हेयोपादेयविरहात् owing to the absence of the rejectable and the acceptable एवं as well as हर्षविषादयो: of joy and sorrow अभावात् because of

absence अद्य today अहम् I एवम् thus एव verily आस्थित:
abide.

4. Having[1] nothing to accept and nothing to
reject, and having neither joy nor sorrow, thus,[2]
sir, do I now firmly abide.

[1] *Having etc.*—Acceptance or rejection and joy or
sorrow are possible only when we identify ourselves
with sense-objects and create distinctions. But the Self
is One, perfect, and all-pervasive, and has therefore
nothing to lose or gain and thereby suffer misery or feel
happy.

[2] *Thus*—as perfect and all-pervasive.

आश्रमानाश्रमं ध्यानं चित्तस्वीकृतवर्जनम् ।
विकल्पं मम वीक्ष्यैतैरेवमेवाहमास्थित: ॥ ५ ॥

आश्रमानाश्रमं A stage of life or no stage of life ध्यानं
meditation चित्तस्वीकृतवर्जनम् control of mental functions
एतै: by these मम my विकल्पं distraction वीक्ष्य seeing एवम्
thus एव verily अहम् I आस्थित: abide.

5. A stage[1] of life or no stage of life, meditation,
control of mental functions—finding[2] that these
cause distraction to me, thus[3] verily do I firmly
abide.

[1] *Stage*—refers to the traditional four stages of life
with their graded duties and modes of living—Brahma-
carya (student life), Gārhasthya (life of a householder),
Vānaprastha (hermit's life), and Sannyāsa (life of one who
completely renounces the world and its attachments).

[2] *Finding etc.*—All these have reference to body and
mind, but the Self transcends them. Hence they are distractions to a man of Self-knowledge.

[3] *Thus*—free from all such distractions.

कर्मानुष्ठानमज्ञानाद्यथैवोपरमस्तथा ।
बुध्वा सम्यगिदं तत्त्वमेवमेवाहमास्थितः ॥ ६ ॥

यथा As कर्मानुष्ठानम् performance of action अज्ञानात्
from ignorance (भवति is) तथा एव even so उपरमः cessation (अज्ञानात् भवति) इदं this तत्त्वम् truth सम्यक् fully बुध्वा
knowing अहम् I एवम् thus एव verily आस्थितः abide.

6. Abstention[1] from action is as much the
outcome of ignorance as the performance of action.
Knowing this truth fully well, thus[2] do I firmly
abide.

[1] *Abstention etc.*—Both performance of and abstention
from work presuppose consciousness of the ego and the
external and internal worlds, and this is ignorance.

[2] *Thus*—in the Self in which there can be no question
of action or abstention from it.

अचिन्त्यं चिन्त्यमानोऽपि चिन्तारूपं भजत्यसौ ।
त्यक्त्वा तद्भावनं तस्मादेवमेवाहमास्थितः ॥ ७ ॥

अचिन्त्यं The unthinkable चिन्त्यमानः thinking अपि
even असौ one चिन्तारूपं a form of thought भजति has recourse to तस्मात् so तत् that भावनं thought त्यक्त्वा giving up
अहम् I एवम् thus एव certainly आस्थितः abide.

7. Thinking[1] on the Unthinkable One, one only
has recourse to a form of thought. Therefore giving
up that thought, thus[2] do I firmly abide.

[1] *Thinking etc.*—The Self is beyond thought and cannot be an object of thought. Meditating on It is therefore
nothing but creating a certain mode of mind, and that

is not Brahman. To realize Brahman, one must go beyond the limitations of the mind and become Brahman Itself.

² *Thus*—beyond thought.

एवमेव कृतं येन स कृतार्थो भवेदसौ ।
एवमेव स्वभावो यः स कृतार्थो भवेदसौ ॥ ८ ॥

येन By whom एवम् thus एव even कृतं accomplished स: असौ he कृतार्थ: fulfilled भवेत् becomes य: who एवम् स्वभाव: of such nature एव verily स: असौ he कृतार्थ: fulfilled भवेत् becomes.

8. Blessed is the man who[1] has accomplished this. Blessed is he who[2] is such by nature.

¹ *Who etc.*—Who, through *sādhanā*, has realized the Self as beyond all actions, physical and mental.

² *Who etc.*—indicates a higher stage. The absolute state is natural to him now.

CHAPTER XIII

HAPPINESS

जनक उवाच ।

अकिञ्चनभवं स्वास्थ्यं कौपीनत्वेऽपि दुर्लभम् ।
त्यागादाने विहायास्मादहमासे यथासुखम् ॥ १ ॥

जनक: Janaka उवाच said :

अकिञ्चनभवं Born of the consciousness that nothing else exists स्वास्थ्यं tranquillity कौपीनत्वे in the state of having a loin-cloth अपि even दुर्लभम् rare अस्मात् therefore त्यागादाने renunciation and acceptance विहाय giving up अहम् I यथासुखम् happily आसे live.

Janaka said:

1. The tranquillity[1] which is born of the consciousness that there is nothing but the Self is rare[2] even for one who wears but a loin-cloth. Therefore,[3] giving up renunciation and acceptance, I live happily.

[1] *Tranquillity—Svāsthya*, which literally means the state of being established in the Self.

[2] *Rare etc.*—A very high state of spiritual realization is indicated. Even the wearing of a loin-cloth is indicative of relative consciousness.

[3] *Therefore etc.*—Renunciation no less than acceptance presupposes egoism and attachment, which spring from ignorance. True happiness, therefore, consists in transcending them both.

कुत्रापि खेदः कायस्य जिह्वा कुत्रापि खिद्यते ।
मनः कुत्रापि तत्त्यक्ता पुरुषार्थे स्थितः सुखम् ॥ २ ॥

कुत्र अपि Somewhere कायस्य of body खेदः distress
(भवति is) कुत्र अपि somewhere जिह्वा tongue खिद्यते is
fatigued कुत्र अपि somewhere मनः mind (खिद्यते is tired)
तत् this त्यक्ता forgoing (अहं I) पुरुषार्थे in life's goal सुखम्
happily स्थितः established (अस्मि am).

2. There is trouble of the body[1] here, trouble
of the tongue[2] there, and trouble of the mind[3] else-
where. Having renounced these, in life's[4] supreme
goal I live happily.

[1] *Body*—in the practice of penances etc.

[2] *Tongue*—in the study of scriptures etc.

[3] *Mind*—in meditation etc.

The application of body, speech, and mind for
Self-realization presupposes imperfection—the Self has
not yet been realized. This is the period of struggle.
Cessation of striving and complete detachment come with
complete Self-realization. Being established in the perfection of the eternal Self, the seer knows himself as
distinct from all his actions, physical, vocal, and mental,
and is, therefore, completely detached and truly inactive.

[4] *Life's etc.*—Self-realization or *mokṣa*.

कृतं किमपि नैव स्यादिति सञ्चिन्त्य तत्त्वतः ।
यदा यत् कर्तुमायाति तत्कृत्वासे यथासुखम् ॥ ३ ॥

तत्त्वतः In reality (आत्मना by the Self) किमपि anything
whatever एव certainly न not कृतं done स्यात् is इति this
सञ्चिन्त्य thinking fully यदा when यत् what कर्तुम् to do

आयाति comes तत् that कृत्वा doing (अहं I) यथासुखम्
happily आसे live.

3. Fully realizing that nothing[1] whatsoever is
really done by the Self, I do[2] whatever[3] presents
itself to be done and so I live happily.

[1] *Nothing etc.*—Because whatever is done is done by
the body, mind, and senses accompanied by the ego.
The Self is beyond all these.

[2] *Do*—being devoid of the ego and being unattached.
The body and mind work, the Self remains unattached.

[3] *Whatever etc.*—as a result of past actions which are
responsible for the present body.

कर्मनैष्कर्म्यनिर्बन्धभावा देहस्थयोगिनः ।
संयोगायोगविरहादहमासे यथासुखम् ॥ ४ ॥

देहस्थयोगिनः The *yogins* who are attached to the
body कर्मनैष्कर्म्यनिर्बन्धभावाः who insist upon action or inaction (भवन्ति are) अहम् I संयोगायोगविरहात् owing to the
absence of association and dissociation यथासुखम् happily
आसे live.

4. The *yogins* who are attached to the body
insist upon action[1] or inaction. Owing to the
absence[2] of association and dissociation, I live
happily.

[1] *Action etc.*—Action and inaction are true only for
those who still have the body-idea. To one who is without this, they are meaningless.

[2] *Absence etc.*—due to complete disidentification of
the body, mind, and senses from the Self.

अर्थानर्थौ न मे स्थित्या गत्या न शयनेन वा ।
तिष्ठन् गच्छन् स्वपन् तस्मादहमासे यथासुखम् ॥ ५ ॥

स्थित्या By staying मे my अर्थानर्थौ good or evil न not
(स्त: are) गत्या by going शयनेन by sleeping वा or न not
(मे my अर्थानर्थौ good or harm स्त: are) तस्मात् so अहम्
I तिष्ठन् staying गच्छन् going स्वपन् sleeping यथासुखम्
happily आसे live.

5. No[1] good or evil accrues to me by staying,
going, or sleeping. So, whether[2] I stay, go, or sleep,
I live happily.

[1] *No etc.*—Good and evil are the results of actions
done by the body and mind. The results of action do not
affect one who is not attached to the body and mind.

[2] *Whether etc.*—So long as one is in the body, one
does various actions. But they make no difference to the
inner consciousness of the man of Self-knowledge, as they
do in the case of the ignorant man.

स्वपतो नास्ति मे हानिः सिद्धियँत्नवतो न वा ।
नाशोल्लासौ विहायास्मादहमासे यथासुखम् ॥ ६ ॥

स्वपत: Sleeping मे my हानि: loss न not अस्ति is यत्नवत:
striving (मे my) वा or सिद्धि: success न not (अस्ति is)
अस्मात् so नाशोल्लासौ loss and elation विहाय forgoing अहम्
I यथासुखम् happily आसे live.

6. I do not lose by sleeping[1] nor gain by
striving. So, giving up thoughts of loss[2] and elation,[3]
I live happily.

[1] *Sleeping*—that is, when inactive.

² *Loss*—of pleasure because nothing has been acquir-
ed.

³ *Elation*—due to the acquisition of worldly things.

सुखादिरूपानियमं भावेष्वालोक्य भूरिशः ।
शुभाशुभे विहायास्मादहमासे यथासुखम् ॥ ७ ॥

भावेषु In different conditions सुखादिरूपानियमं inconstancy of the forms of pleasure etc. भूरिशः repeatedly
आलोक्य observing अस्मात् so अहम् I शुभाशुभे good and evil
विहाय renouncing यथासुखम् happily आसे live.

7. Observing again and again the inconstancy
of pleasure and pain under different circumstances,
I have renounced¹ good and evil, and I live happily.

¹ *Renounced etc.*—Good and evil are associated in our
minds with happiness and sorrow. We seek good and
avoid evil in order to be happy. But one who has realized
that happiness and sorrow are really the products of
circumstances, changing with their changes, and are not
of the eternal Self, no longer cares for good or evil and
remains established in the Self, in which alone there is
real and absolute happiness.

CHAPTER XIV

TRANQUILLITY

जनक उवाच ।

प्रकृत्या शून्यचित्तो यः प्रमादाद्भावभावनः ।
निद्रितो बोधित इव क्षीणसंस्मरणो हि सः ॥ १ ॥

जनकः Janaka उवाच said :

यः Who प्रकृत्या by nature शून्यचित्तः empty-minded
प्रमादात् through inadvertence भावभावनः thinking of objects
निद्रितः asleep (अपि though) बोधितः awake इव as if सः
he हि verily क्षीणसंस्मरणः one whose recollections (of
worldly life) are exhausted.

Janaka said :

1. He verily has his recollections[1] of worldly
life exhausted,[2] who is empty-minded[3] by[4] nature,
who thinks[5] of sense-objects involuntarily, and who
is, as[6] it were, awake though asleep.

[1] *Recollections etc.*—implying the bondage of *karma*,
effects of past good and evil actions, and consequent
birth and rebirth.

[2] *Exhausted*—For him effects of past actions are
destroyed for ever. Their forces have no longer any hold
on him and his present actions also do not leave any
effect upon his mind.

[3] *Empty-minded*—devoid of any desires or *saṁskāras*,
impressions, and knowledge of objects, but full of the
luminous consciousness of the Self alone.

[4] *By nature*—in reality.

[5] *Thinks etc.*—So long as his body remains, he becomes casually conscious of the phenomenal world, due to the remnants of *karma,* called *prārabdha karma,* which still continue to function. But that consciousness of objects is not the same as an ordinary man's consciousness of them, for with the man of realization it is apparent and unsubstantial. It is only illusory and does not leave any effect. Hence, *in reality* he is empty-minded.

[6] *As etc.*—Sleep generally clouds our consciousness. But the man of realization is ever full of the knowledge of the Self and it is not obstructed even when he is asleep.

क धनानि क मित्राणि क मे विषयदस्यवः ।

क शास्त्रं क च विज्ञानं यदा मे गलिता स्पृहा ॥ २ ॥

यदा When मे my स्पृहा desire गलिता has melted away (तदा then) मे my क़ु where धनानि riches क़ु where मित्राणि friends क़ु where विषयदस्यवः robbers in the form of sense-objects क़ु where शास्त्रं scripture क़ु where विज्ञानं knowledge च and.

2. When desire[1] has melted away, where then are my riches, where my friends, where are the robbers[2] in the form of sense-objects, where[3] the scriptures, and where knowledge?[4]

[1] *Desire*—for the objects of enjoyment in this world or the next.

[2] *Robbers etc.*—Because the objects of the senses rob us of the perception of the Self.

[3] *Where etc.*—Scriptural injunctions are only for those who are still in ignorance. They are of no use to a man of Self-realization.

[4] *Knowledge*—secular as well as scriptural. The one is derived from worldly experience and is therefore of no

use to a *jñānin*; while the other, being indirect knowledge of spiritual realities, is no longer required because he has now directly experienced them.

विज्ञाते साक्षिपुरुषे परमात्मनि चेश्वरे ।
नैराश्ये बन्धमोक्षे च न चिन्ता मुक्तये मम ॥ ३ ॥

साक्षिपुरुषे Self who is the witness ईश्वरे Lord च and परमात्मनि the Supreme Self विज्ञाते (सति) having been realized बन्धमोक्षे in bondage and liberation च and नैराश्ये desirelessness (सति being) मुक्तये for emancipation मम my चिन्ता anxiety न not (अस्ति is).

3. As I have realized the Supreme Self who is the Witness and the Lord, and have[1] become indifferent to both bondage and liberation, I feel no anxiety for emancipation.

[1] *Have etc.*—because of the realization of the eternal, ever-free, and ever-blissful Ātman. A man of Self-realization transcends all consciousness of bondage and freedom. It is only the ignorant man who wants to shake off bondage and attain emancipation.

अन्तर्विकल्पशून्यस्य बहिः स्वच्छन्दचारिणः ।
भ्रान्तस्येव दशास्तास्तास्ताद‍शा एव जानते ॥ ४ ॥

अन्तः Within विकल्पशून्यस्य devoid of doubts बहिः outside भ्रान्तस्य इव like a deluded one स्वच्छन्दचारिणः of one who moves at his own pleasure ताः ताः such and such दशाः conditions ताद‍शाः those like him एव surely जानते know.

4. The different conditions of one who within

is devoid[1] of doubts but outwardly moves[2] about at his own pleasure like a deluded person, can[3] only be understood by those like him.

[1] *Devoid etc.*—He has perfect Knowledge. He possesses the whole and complete Truth. He is, therefore, free from all doubts and uncertainties.

[2] *Moves etc.*—One who has attained Self-knowledge is no longer bound by man-made laws for the regulation of his conduct which may sometimes appear to be unbecoming or wrong.

[3] *Can etc.*—The ways of a man of Realization can only be understood by another man of Realization. The average person who estimates people by their outward conduct can never understand men of Self-knowledge, for their external ways are no sure clue to their inner illumination.

CHAPTER XV

KNOWLEDGE OF THE SELF

अष्टावक्र उवाच ।

यथातथोपदेशेन कृतार्थः सत्त्वबुद्धिमान् ।
आजीवमपि जिज्ञासुः परस्तत्र विमुह्यति ॥ १ ॥

अष्टावक्रः Aṣṭāvakra उवाच said:

सत्त्वबुद्धिमान् A man of pure intellect यथातथा in whatever manner उपदेशेन by instruction कृतार्थः (स्यात्) gains his end परः the other आजीवम् throughout life जिज्ञासुः desirous to know अपि even तत्र there विमुह्यति is bewildered.

Aṣṭāvakra said:

1. A man of pure[1] intellect realizes the Self even by instruction casually[2] imparted. A man of impure intellect is bewildered[3] in trying to realize the Self even after enquiring throughout life.

[1] *Pure etc.*—Self-knowledge instantaneously dawns upon one who has completely purified his intellect by undergoing the necessary disciplines and endowing himself with the four qualifications required (see Chap. I, verse 1, note 3). 'Pure' indicates that the intellect has been freed from the elements of *rajas* (passion) and *tamas* (darkness) and is full of *sattva* (light).

[2] *Casually etc.*—whenever and in whatever manner instruction on the Self is imparted to him by the Guru. A little instruction is enough for a qualified disciple.

³ *Bewildered*—Because an unqualified aspirant mis-conceives the nature of the Ātman. Only a purified intellect can conceive it.

मोक्षो विषयवैरस्यं बन्धो वैषयिको रसः ।
एतावदेव विज्ञानं यथेच्छसि तथा कुरु ॥ २ ॥

विषयवैरस्यं Distaste for sense-objects मोक्ष: liberation (भवति is) वैषयिक: sensual रस: attachment बन्ध: bondage (भवति is) एतावत् of such kind एव verily विज्ञानं Knowledge (भवति is) यथा as (त्वम् you) इच्छसि wish तथा so कुरु do.

2. Non-attachment for sense-objects is liberation; love for sense-objects is bondage. Such verily is Knowledge. Now do as you please.

Aṣṭāvakra tersely describes the essential nature of liberation and of bondage, and points out the sole duty of the aspirant.

वाग्मिप्राज्ञमहोद्योगं जनं मूकजडालसम् ।
करोति तत्त्वबोधोऽयमतस्त्यक्तो बुभुक्षुभिः ॥ ३ ॥

अयम् This तत्त्वबोध: knowledge of the Truth वाग्मि-प्राज्ञमहोद्योगं eloquent, wise, and active जनं man मूकजडालसम् mute, inert, and inactive करोति makes अत: so बुभुक्षुभि: by those who want to enjoy त्यक्त: is shunned.

3. This knowledge of the Truth makes¹ an eloquent, wise, and active person mute, inert, and inactive. Therefore it is shunned² by those who want to enjoy the world.

¹ *Makes etc.*—This passage should not be understood
literally. All talking, knowledge, and activities have
attainable objects in view. When the Self who is the All
and the Whole is realized, nothing remains to be attained,
and hence all talking, knowing, and doing cease and the
aspirant becomes silent, inert, and inactive. This is a sign
of the highest realization. Mere outward silence and
inactivity are nothing. They must be the outcome of
deep realization.

² *Shunned*—Because worldly enjoyment is impossible
ir that high spiritual state. The mentality of a worldly
person is diametrically opposed to that of a Knower of
the Self.

न त्वं देहो न ते देहो भोक्ता कर्ता न वा भवान् ।
चिद्रूपोऽसि सदा साक्षी निरपेक्षः सुखं चर ॥ ४ ॥

त्वं You देह: body न not ते your देह: body न not
भवान् you कर्ता doer भोक्ता enjoyer वा or न not (त्वं you)
चिद्रूप: Consciousness itself सदा ever साक्षी Witness निरपेक्ष:
free असि are सुखं happily चर move.

4. You are not the body, nor is the body yours;
you are not the doer nor the enjoyer. You are
Consciousness itself, the eternal Witness, and free.
Go about happily.

रागद्वेषौ मनोधर्मौ न मनस्ते कदाचन ।
निर्विकल्पोऽसि बोधात्मा निर्विकारः सुखं चर ॥ ५ ॥

रागद्वेषौ Attachment and abhorrence मनोधर्मौ attributes of mind (भवत: are) मन: mind कदाचन ever ते your
न not (भवति is त्वं you) निर्विकल्प: free from conflict

बोधात्मा Intelligence itself निर्विकार: changeless असि are सुखं happily चर move.

5. Attachment and abhorrence are attributes of the mind. The mind is never yours. You are Intelligence itself, free from conflict, and changeless. Go about happily.

The aspirant should neither love nor hate. To do so is to identify one's self with the mind and thus lose the awareness of one's true nature. Narrow, selfish love is an obstruction to Self-realization, but not universal love which grows only out of true knowledge of the eternal Self.

सर्वभूतेषु चात्मानं सर्वभूतानि चात्मनि ।
विज्ञाय निरहंकारो निर्ममस्त्वं सुखी भव ॥ ६ ॥

सर्वभूतेषु In all beings च (expletive) आत्मानं Self सर्वभूतानि all beings च also आत्मनि in Self विज्ञाय knowing निरहंकार: free from egoism निर्मम: free from the sense of 'mine' त्वं you सुखी happy भव be.

6. Realizing the Self[1] in all and all[2] in the Self, free from egoism and free from the sense of 'mine', be happy.

[1] Self etc.—as substratum.

[2] All etc.—as superimposed on the Self.

On realizing the Self, the aspirant actually feels that he is the essence and reality of all things and that all things exist in him. Our present consciousness of our limitations and of our separateness from all other beings and things is due to our identification with the mind which, with its categories of time, space, and causation, has created various forms. Disidentify yourself from the

mind, and these forms will vanish and only the One will
remain, which is both yourself and the whole universe.

विश्वं स्फुरति यत्रेदं तरङ्गा इव सागरे ।
तत्त्वमेव न सन्देहश्चिन्मूर्ते विज्वरो भव ॥ ७ ॥

यत्र In which इदं this विश्वं universe सागरे in the
ocean तरङ्गाः waves इव like स्फुरति is manifested तत् that
त्वम् you एव verily (असि are) न not सन्देहः doubt चिन्मूर्ते
O you Intelligence विज्वरः free from fever भव be.

7. You are indeed That in which the universe
manifests itself like waves on the ocean. O you
Intelligence, be[1] you free from the fever[2] of the mind.

[1]*Be etc.*—When one realizes that the Self is the only
substance pervading the universe, and that the universe
is no other than the Self, one does not hanker after
worldly objects nor become in any way entangled by
them.

[2] *Fever etc.*—desire for the enjoyment of worldly
objects, and all the complications that arise out of ignorance of the true nature of the Self.

श्रद्धस्व तात श्रद्धस्व नात्र मोहं कुरुष्व भोः ।
ज्ञानस्वरूपो भगवानात्मा त्वं प्रकृतेः परः ॥ ८ ॥

भोः तात O child श्रद्धस्व have faith श्रद्धस्व have faith
अत्र in this मोहं confusion न not कुरुष्व make त्वं you
ज्ञानस्वरूपः Knowledge itself भगवान् Lord आत्मा Self प्रकृतेः
परः beyond nature (असि are).

8. Have[1] faith, my son, have faith. Never[2]
confuse yourself in this. You are Knowledge itself,

you are the Lord, you are the Self, and you are
beyond[3] Nature.

[1] *Have etc.*—Aṣṭāvakra is impressing the true nature
of the Self on the mind of the disciple.

[2] *Never etc.*—Till one has actually realized the Self,
it is hard to believe that the Self is really what the seers
describe it to be and that the universe is really nothing.
Hence faith, the grasp upon the ultimate, is the condition
precedent for a seeker of Truth.

[3] *Beyond etc.*—unaffected by Nature.

गुणैः संवेष्टितो देहस्तिष्ठत्यायाति याति च ।

आत्मा न गन्ता नागन्ता किमेनमनुशोचसि ॥ ९ ॥

गुणैः By the constituents of nature संवेष्टितः enclosed
देहः body आयाति comes तिष्ठति stays याति goes च and
आत्मा Self न not गन्ता goes न not आगन्ता comes किम् why
एनम् it अनुशोचसि lament.

9. The body, composed[1] of the ingredients of
nature, comes, stays, and goes. The Self[2] neither
comes nor goes. Why, then, do you mourn it?

[1] *Composed etc.*—Prakṛti (nature) is constituted of
three ingredients called *guṇas*, viz. *sattva*, *rajas*, and *tamas*,
i.e. goodness, passion, and darkness. All creation evolves
from nature and therefore partakes of these three constituents.

[2] *Self etc.*—The Self is distinct from the body and
does not partake of its nature. The body changes, the
Self does not.

देहस्तिष्ठतु कल्पान्तं गच्छत्वद्यैव वा पुनः ।

क्व वृद्धिः क्व च वा हानिस्तव चिन्मात्ररूपिणः ॥ १० ॥

देहः Body कल्पान्तं to the end of the cycle तिष्ठतु let

remain पुन: again अद्य today एव verily गच्छतु let go वा
or चिन्मात्ररूपिण: तव of you who are Pure Intelligence
कृ where वृद्धि: increase. कृ where च (expletive) वा or
हानि: decrease.

10. Let the body last to the end of the *kalpa*
(cycle) or let it go even today. Where[1] is there any
increase or decrease in you who are Pure Intelligence?

[1] *Where etc.*—The varying conditions of the body do
not make the slightest difference to the Self which is
immutable.

त्वय्यनन्तमहाम्भोधौ विश्ववीचि: स्वभावत: ।
उदेतु वास्तमायातु न ते वृद्धिर्न वा क्षति: ॥ ११ ॥

अनन्तमहाम्भोधौ The infinite ocean त्वयि in you विश्व-
वीचि: the wave of the universe स्वभावत: spontaneously
उदेतु let rise अस्तम् आयातु let subside वा or ते your वृद्धि:
increase न not (भवति is) क्षति: loss वा or न not (भवति is).

11. In you who are the infinite ocean, let the
waves of the universe rise or fall according to their
own nature. That means no gain[1] or loss to you.

[1] *Gain etc.*—Just as waves when they arise do not add
to the ocean, or subtract from it when they subside, so
the creation of the universe does not add anything to the
Self, nor does it take anything away from It when it is
dissolved. The universe is endlessly going through creation and dissolution. But that does not affect the Self.
The Self is beyond time and causation. Creation and
dissolution are in time. They are only superimpositions.
The Self is infinite. In reality nothing else exists.

तात चिन्मात्ररूपोऽसि न ते भिन्नमिदं जगत् ।
अतः कस्य कथं कुत्र हेयोपादेयकल्पना ॥ १२ ॥

तात Child (त्वं you) चिन्मात्ररूप: Pure Intelligence
itself असि are इदं this जगत् world ते from you भिन्नम्
different न not (भवति is) अतः therefore कस्य whose
कथ॑ how कुत्र where हेयोपादेयकल्पना the thought of the
rejectable and the acceptable.

12. My child, you are Pure Intelligence itself.
This universe is nothing different[1] from you. Therefore[2] how and where can anyone have the idea of
acceptance and rejection?

[1] *Different etc.*—When we try to grasp the reality of
the universe, we find it to be our own Self, which is
pure Intelligence itself.

[2] *Therefore etc.*—If we know the universe as our own
Self, which is Pure Intelligence, the distinctions of good
or bad in the universe cannot arise. I alone exist. I cannot reject or accept myself. There is no instrument, the
mind, for such rejection or acceptance. And there is no
space or reality outside me where I can accept or where
I can reject. Aṣṭāvakra urges us to outgrow the present
limited and distorted vision.

एकस्मिन्नव्यये शान्ते चिदाकाशोऽमले त्वयि ।
कुतो जन्म कुतः कर्म कुतोऽहंकार एव च ॥ १३ ॥

एकस्मिन् One अव्यये undecaying शान्ते calm अमले
pure चिदाकाशे the space which is Consciousness त्वयि in
you जन्म birth कुत: from where कर्म action कुत: from
where अहंकार: egoism एव even कुत: wherefrom च and.

13. From where will there be birth,[1] action,[2]

and even egoism[3] for you who are One, immutable, calm, stainless, and Pure[4] Consciousness?

[1] *Birth*—One who is self-existent and immutable cannot be born.

[2] *Action*—Action implies change and the desire to gain something which is not in one's possession. But the man of Realization knows himself as the Self which is One, calm, perfect, and self-contained. He has nothing outside himself to strive for.

[3] *Egoism*—Egoism is the first offspring of ignorance. Egoism produces the sense of duality, which, in turn, manifests the manifold universe. The whole of creation is thus an illusion. It is superimposed on the Self which is One and all-pervasive. As such, the whole creation, from egoism to the manifold universe, has no existence other than the Self itself.

[4] *Pure etc.*—Literally, the space of Intelligence. Space is here identical with *Cit*, Pure Intelligence. *Cit* has been conceived as *ākāśa*, space, because, like *ākāśa*, it is all-pervasive and unaffected. Also, all perception requires, as an essential factor, the existence of *ākāśa*. Therefore three different *ākāśas* have been conceived: (1) *mahākāśa*, the great space, which is the ordinary space in which we perceive external objects; (2) *cittākāśa*, the mental space; everything that we imagine, dream, or supersensibly perceive is in the mental space; and (3) *cidākāśa*, the Intelligence space, the space in which the Self perceives itself; here space is not something different from the perceiver and the perceived, as in the other two *ākāśas*, for in Self-perception it is all one, there is neither subject nor object; hence space is here identical with the Self. Really speaking, in Self-perception there is no space; but the word 'space' is used to extend the analogy of the other two kinds of perception to Self-perception.

यत्त्वं पश्यसि तत्रैकस्त्वमेव प्रतिभाससे ।

किं पृथक् भासते स्वर्णात् कटकाङ्गदनूपुरम् ॥ १४ ॥

यत् What त्वं you पश्यसि see तत्र there एक: alone त्वम्
you एव verily प्रतिभाससे appear कटकाङ्गदनूपुरम् bracelets,
armlets, and anklets किम् (interrogative) स्वर्णात् from
gold पृथक् different भासते appear.

14. You alone appear as whatever you perceive.
Do bracelets, armlets, and anklets appear different
from gold?

The Self is the only reality and the universe is no
other than the Self itself—only names and forms have
been superimposed on it. Just as the reality of gold
ornaments is gold itself and nothing but gold, so is the
reality of the universe not different from the Self. The
Self alone exists.

अयं सोऽहमयं नाहं विभागमिति सन्त्यज ।
सर्वमात्मेति निश्चित्य निःसङ्कल्पः सुखी भव ॥ १५ ॥

अहम् I अयं (pleonastic) सः He अहं I अयं this न not
(अस्मि am) इति this विभागम् distinction सन्त्यज give up
completely आत्मा Self सर्वं all इति this निश्चित्य realizing
ʳनःसङ्कल्पः free from desire सुखी happy भव be.

15. Completely give up such distinctions as 'I
am He'[1] and 'I am not this'.[2] Consider all[3] as the
Self and be desireless and happy.

Aṣṭāvakra emphasizes that the Transcendental
Reality and the universe are not different. The distinction is born of ignorance. The universe has no separate
existence apart from the Self.

[1] *He*—the transcendental Self.

[2] *This*—the universe.

[3] *All*—reality, both transcendental and relative.

तवैवाज्ञानतो विश्वं त्वमेकः परमार्थतः ।
त्वत्तोऽन्यो नास्ति संसारी नासंसारी च कश्चन ॥ १६ ॥

तव Your अज्ञानतः through ignorance एव alone विश्वं
universe (भवति is) परमार्थतः in reality त्वम् you एकः One
त्वत्तः than you अन्यः other कश्चन any संसारी transmigratory (*jīva*) न not अस्ति is असंसारी non-transmigratory
(transcendental Self) च and न not (अस्ति is).

16. It is through your ignorance alone that the
universe exists. In reality you are One. There is
no individual self or Supreme Self other than you.

So long as the universe exists, the Self is conceived
in two aspects—individual and absolute. In the individual aspect it is transmigratory, *saṃsārin,* passing
through rounds of births and rebirths. In the absolute
aspect it is eternal and unchanging. But the universe
exists only through ignorance. In reality, the Self is One;
the universe does not exist. So the distinction between the
individual and absolute aspects of the Self is *ipso facto*
unreal. The Self alone is.

भ्रान्तिमात्रमिदं विश्वं न किञ्चिदिति निश्चयी ।
निर्वासनः स्फूर्तिमात्रो न किञ्चिदिव शाम्यति ॥ १७ ॥

इदं This विश्वं universe भ्रान्तिमात्रम् mere illusion न
not किञ्चित् anything इति this निश्चयी one who knows
for certain निर्वासनः desireless स्फूर्तिमात्रः Intelligence itself
(सन् being) न not किञ्चित् anything (अस्ति exists) इव
as if शाम्यति finds peace.

17. One who knows for certain that this universe is but an illusion and a nothing, becomes

desireless and Pure Intelligence, and finds peace as[1]
if nothing exists.

[1] *As etc.*—See Chapter XI, verse 8, note 2.

एक एव भवाम्भोधावासीदस्ति भविष्यति ।
न ते बन्धोऽस्ति मोक्षो वा कृतकृत्यः सुखं चर ॥ १८ ॥

भवाम्भोधौ In the ocean of the world एक: one एव
only आसीत् was अस्ति is भविष्यति will be ते your बन्ध:
bondage मोक्ष: liberation वा or न not अस्ति is कृतकृत्य:
contented सुखं happily चर move.

18. In the ocean of the world One only was, is,
and will be. You have neither bondage[1] nor liberation. Live contented[2] and happily.

[1] *Bondage etc.*—Bondage or freedom cannot be predicated of the Self which is One without a second, and
which alone exists for all time.

[2] *Contented*—Because there is nothing to desire.

मा सङ्कल्पविकल्पाभ्यां चित्तं क्षोभय चिन्मय ।
उपशाम्य सुखं तिष्ठ स्वात्मन्यानन्दविग्रहे ॥ १९ ॥

चिन्मय O Pure Intelligence संकल्पविकल्पाभ्यां by
affirmations and negations चित्त॑ mind मा not क्षोभय
disturb उपशाम्य be calm आनन्दविग्रहे embodiment of bliss
स्वात्मनि in your own self सुखं happily तिष्ठ abide.

19. O Pure Intelligence, do not disturb your
mind with affirmations and negations. Be calm and
abide happily in your own self which is Bliss itself.

त्यजैव ध्यानं सर्वत्र मा किञ्चिद्धृदि धारय ।
आत्मा त्वं मुक्त एवासि किं विमृश्य करिष्यसि ॥ २० ॥

सर्वत्र In every way ध्यानं thinking एव even त्यज
give up हृदि in the mind किञ्चित् anything मा not धारय
hold त्वं you आत्मा Self मुक्तः free एव verily असि are
विमृश्य thinking किं what करिष्यसि will do.

20. Completely give up even contemplation
and hold nothing in your mind. You are verily the
Self, free. What will you do by thinking?

Contemplation presupposes duality of consciousness
which, born of ignorance, is the very antithesis of the
nature of the Self. Aṣṭāvakra therefore instructs the
aspirant to dwell in the consciousness of the eternal
Self, which is One and ever free.

CHAPTER XVI

SPECIAL INSTRUCTION

अष्टावक्र उवाच ।

आचक्ष्व शृणु वा तात नानाशास्त्राण्यनेकशः ।
तथापि न तव स्वास्थ्यं सर्वविस्मरणाद्दते ॥ १ ॥

अष्टावक्रः Aṣṭāvakra उवाच said:

तात Child नानाशास्त्राणि diverse scriptures अनेकशः
many times आचक्ष्व speak शृणु hear वा or तथापि still सर्व-
विस्मरणात् through forgetting all द्दते except तव your
स्वास्थ्यं Self-abidance न not (अस्ति is).

Aṣṭāvakra said:

1. My child, you may often speak[1] upon
various scriptures or hear them. But cannot be
established[2] in the Self unless you forget[3] all.

The central point of Aṣṭāvakra's teaching is that the
Self alone exists and that all else is false, unreal. The
unreal, manifold universe is constantly engaging our
minds and hence we cannot have knowledge of the Self.
To be fully established in the Self, the position must be
reversed.

[1] *Speak etc.*—The *Śruti* repeatedly says that 'the Self
is not to be realized by the power of speech, by a vast
intellect, or by the study of the Vedas'. It is a question of
actual experience and not of mere intellectual knowledge.

[2] *Established etc.*—when the self knows the Self and
nothing else. In our present condition, we are not in

our own Self. We are conscious only of the body and mind and the various things of the world. Wherever our consciousness is, there we are.

[3] *Forget etc.*—That is, one must be conscious of the Self alone and should perceive everything else as nothing but the Self itself. This is a state which is attained by destroying ignorance which is the cause of the manifold universe. A state of deep sleep or a similar condition induced artificially, in which all is forgotten, is not meant because even in that state ignorance still remains and the manifold universe reappears as soon as one awakes.

भोगं कर्म समाधिं वा कुरु विज्ञ तथापि ते ।
चित्तं निरस्तसर्वाशमत्यर्थं रोचयिष्यति ॥ २ ॥

विज्ञ O wise one भोगं enjoyment कर्म work समाधिं mental concentration वा or कुरु do तथापि yet ते your चित्तं mind निरस्तसर्वाशम् in which all desires are extinguished अत्यर्थं that which is beyond objects रोचयिष्यति will yearn for.

2. O wise one, you may enjoy,[1] or work, or practise mental concentration. But your mind will still yearn[2] for your own true nature which is beyond all objects and in which all desires are extinguished.

[1] *Enjoy etc.*—All these occupations indicate that the Self has not yet been realized.

[2] *Yearn etc.*—Because one cannot enjoy everlasting bliss except in the realization of one's own true nature.

आयासात् सकलो दुःखी नैनं जानाति कश्चन ।
अनेनैवोपदेशेन धन्यः प्राप्नोति निर्वृतिम् ॥ ३ ॥

सकलः All आयासात् from effort दुःखी miserable कश्चन

anyone एनं this न not जानाति knows अनेन this उपदेशेन by instruction एव alone धन्य: blessed one निर्वृंतिम् emancipation प्राप्नोति attains.

3. All are unhappy because[1] they exert themselves. But none knows this.[2] The blessed one attains emancipation through[3] this instruction alone.

[1] *Because etc.*—All exertion presupposes desire—the desire to attain things not possessed at present. Desire, both satisfied and unsatisfied, is the cause of misery. Satisfied desire produces at first satiety and afterwards more desires, and so the chain is lengthened. The unhappiness of unsatisfied desire is obvious.

[2] *This*—that efforts born of desires are the cause of misery.

[3] *Through etc.*—This instruction is enough; for if anyone carries it out in life, that is to say, becomes inactive inwardly by eradicating all desires which are the spring of action, he attains Self-knowledge. Outwardly, however, he may or may not be active. In any case he does not engage himself in any work prompted by inner desires.

व्यापारे खिद्यते यस्तुं निमेषोन्मेषयोरपि ।
तस्यालस्यधुरीणस्य सुखं नान्यस्य कस्यचित् ॥ ४ ॥

य: Who तु (expletive) निमेषोन्मेषयो: of closing and opening the eyelids व्यापारे in the activity अपि even खिद्यते feels pain तस्य आलस्यधुरीणस्य of that master idler सुखं happiness (भवति is) न not अन्यस्य other कस्यचित् of anyone.

4. Happiness belongs to that master idler[1] to

whom even the closing and opening of the eyelids
is an affliction, and to none[2] else.

[1] *Master idler*—The expression refers to the man of
Self-realization, who is completely inactive. He feels even
the little non-volitional action of closing and opening the
eyelids to be a limitation and painful.

[2] *None etc.*—To be truly happy one must be absolutely
detached from physical and mental activity.

इदं कृतमिदं नेति द्वन्द्वैर्मुक्तं यदा मनः ।
धर्मार्थकाममोक्षेषु निरपेक्षं तदा भवेत् ॥ ५ ॥

यदा When मनः mind इदं this कृतम् done इदं this न not
(कृतम् done) इति this द्वन्द्वैः from the pairs of opposites
मुक्तं freed (भवति is) तदा then (मनः mind) धर्मार्थकाममोक्षेषु
in work of religious merit, prosperity, sensual enjoyment
and spiritual emancipation निरपेक्षं indifferent भवेत् becomes.

5. When the mind is free from such[1] pairs of
opposites as 'this is to be done' and 'this is not to be
done', it becomes indifferent[2] to religious merit,
worldly prosperity, sensual enjoyment, and liberation.

[1] *Such etc.*—The idea of duty is meant.

[2] *Indifferent etc.*—The sense of duty arises from desire.
Without desire there cannot be any duty. The four objects
of life, which presuppose desire, are therefore meaningless to a man of true knowledge, for he is free from desire
altogether.

विरक्तो विषयद्वेष्टा रागी विषयलोलुपः ।
ग्रहमोक्षविहीनस्तु न विरक्तो न रागवान् ॥ ६ ॥

विषयद्वेष्टा One who abhors sense-objects विरक्त: unattached (भवति is) विषयलोलुप: one who covets sense-
objects रागी attached (भवति is) ग्रहमोक्षविहीन: one who
does not accept or reject तु but विरक्त: unattached न not
रागवान् attached न not (भवति is).

6. One who abhors sense-objects becomes non-
attached,[1] and one who covets them becomes attached to them. But he[2] who does not accept or reject is
neither unattached nor attached.

[1] *Non-attached*—and therefore renounces. This attempt
at renunciation shows that the aspirant has not realized
all as the Self.

[2] *He etc.*—This indicates a higher state in which all
is realized as the Self. There is therefore no thought of
accepting or rejecting anything.

हेयोपादेयता तावत् संसारविटपांकुर: ।
स्पृहा जीवति याबद्वै निर्विचारदशास्पदम् ॥ ७ ॥

यावत् As long as निर्विचारदशास्पदं the abode of the
state of indiscrimination स्पृहा desire जीवति lives तावत् so
long वै indeed संसारविटपांकुर: the branch and sprout of
the world हेयोपादेयता the sense of the acceptable and the
rejectable (जीवति lives).

7. As long as desire continues, which[1] is the
root of the state of indiscrimination, there will
verily be the sense of attachment[2] and aversion,
which is the branch[3] and shoot of the tree of *saṁsāra*.

[1] *Which etc.*—Desire robs us of the power of understanding the true nature of the world. It makes us consider

the unreal to be real, and the real to be unreal. When desire goes, all things appear to us as they really are.

[2] *Attachment etc.*—wanting certain things and rejecting others.

[3] *Branch etc.*—The trunk and the root of the tree of samsāra (phenomenal life with all its subjective and objective implications) is ignorance. Desire, which makes us want certain things and reject others, is as it were its branches and shoots which make the tree grow more and more. One desire leads to another and thus *karma* grows complex and leads us from birth to death and from death to birth.

प्रवृत्तौ जायते रागो निवृत्तौ द्वेष एव हि ।
निर्द्वन्द्वो बालवद्धीमानेवमेव व्यवस्थितः ॥ ८ ॥

प्रवृत्तौ In activity राग: attachment निवृत्तौ in abstention द्वेष: aversion एव surely हि verily जायते is born धीमान् the man of wisdom बालवत् like a child निर्द्वन्द्व: free from the pairs of opposites (सन् being) एवम् thus एव verily व्यवस्थित: is established.

8. Activity[1] begets attachment; and abstention[2] from it aversion. The man of wisdom is free[3] from the pairs of opposites, like a child, and indeed he lives[4] on like a child.

[1] *Activity*—activity prompted by desire.

[2] *Abstention*—The idea of abstention arises from the consideration that certain things and actions are harmful —hence the feeling of aversion.

[3] *Free etc.*—Activity springing from desire begets attachment for worldly objects, and attachment in its turn leads man from activity to activity, creating for him more and more bondage. Likewise, aversion for sensual

objects begets abstention which in its turn develops more
and more hatred for them. Thus, both these attitudes
frustrate the very purpose which they are intended to
serve. The wise man is therefore indifferent to both
activity and inactivity, and their concomitants—attachment and aversion.

⁴ *Lives etc.*—Not only is he free from the pairs of
opposites inwardly, but his outward life is also like that
of a child—playful, without any set purpose, without
attachment or aversion for anything whatsoever. This is
the highest spiritual state.

हातुमिच्छति संसारं रागी दुःखजिहासया ।
वीतरागो हि निर्दुःखस्तस्मिन्नपि न खिद्यति ॥ ९ ॥

रागी One who is attached दुःखजिहासया wishing to
avoid sorrow संसारं world हातुम् to renounce इच्छति desires वीतराग: one who is free from attachment हि indeed
निर्दुःख: free from sorrow (भवति is) तस्मिन् there अपि even
न not खिद्यति feels miserable.

9. One who is attached to the world wants to
renounce it in¹ order to avoid sorrow. But one²
without attachment is free from sorrow and does
not feel miserable even in the world.

¹ *In etc.*—thinking that the cause of sorrow is in the
world.

² *One etc.*—It is not the world but attachment to it
that is the root of all misery. Free from attachment, one
can live as happily in the world as anywhere else.

यस्याभिमानो मोक्षेऽपि देहेऽपि ममता तथा ।
न च ज्ञानी न वा योगी केवलं दुःखभागसौ ॥ १० ॥

यस्य Whose मोक्षे in liberation अपि even अभिमानः egoistic feeling (or self-conceit) तथा so also देहे in body अपि even ममता sense of 'mine'-ness (अस्ति is) असौ he ज्ञानी wise न not च (expletive) योगी yogin न not वा or केवलं only दुःखभाक् sufferer of misery (भवति is).

10. He who has an egoistic[1] feeling even towards liberation and considers even the body as his own, is neither a *jñānin* nor a *yogin*. He only suffers[2] misery.

[1] *Egoistic etc.*—The word *abhimāna* can be differently interpreted. It may mean simply a reference to egoism, or it may mean actual self-conceit. In. the former sense, the verse would mean: Knowledge, *jñāna*, is a state of complete elimination of the ego. So long as one thinks 'I shall be free', or 'I am free', he holds on to the ego, and has not attained spiritual illumination. In the latter sense, it may mean becoming proud of spiritual achievements. Such pride is, of course, the very antithesis of Knowledge.

[2] *Suffers etc.*—Because he is not free from the sense of 'I' and 'mine' which breeds attachment and is the root cause of all misery.

हरो यद्युपदेष्टा ते हरिः कमलजोऽपि वा ।
तथापि न तव स्वास्थ्यं सर्वविस्मरणाद्दते ॥ ११ ॥

यदि If हरः Hara हरिः Hari कमलजः lotus-born Brahmā वा or अपि even ते your उपदेष्टा instructor (भवति becomes) तथापि yet सर्वविस्मरणात् ऋते without forgetting all तव your स्वास्थ्यं establishment in Self न not (भवति is).

11. Let even[1] Hara, Hari, or the lotus-born

Brahmā be your instructor, but[2] unless[3] you forget all, you cannot be established in the Self.

[1] *Even*—indicating that instruction by such teachers must be very efficacious.

[2] *But*—Even such potent instruction will fail if the supreme condition is not fulfilled.

[3] *Unless etc.*—This is the supreme condition. We must be aware of the Self only, of nothing else. To be aware of anything else is to create a division in consciousness which means we have not realized the Self which is non-differentiated Pure Consciousness.

CHAPTER XVII

THE TRUE KNOWER

अष्टावक्र उवाच ।

तेन ज्ञानफलं प्राप्तं योगाभ्यासफलं तथा ।
तृप्तः स्वच्छेन्द्रियो नित्यमेकाकी रमते तु यः ॥ १ ॥

अष्टावक्रः Aṣṭāvakra उवाच said:

यः Who तु (expletive) तृप्तः contented स्वच्छेन्द्रियः with senses purified (सन् being) नित्यम् ever एकाकी alone रमते enjoys तेन by him ज्ञानफलं the fruit of Knowledge तथा as well as योगाभ्यासफलं the fruit of the practice of Yoga प्राप्तं is gained.

Aṣṭāvakra said:

1. He has gained the fruit of Knowledge as well as of the practice of *yoga*, who, contented[1] and with purified[2] senses, ever enjoys being alone.[3]

[1] *Contented*—wanting nothing, knowing himself as all.

[2] *Purified etc.*—not being attached to any object. So long as the senses are attached to their objects they are impure.

[3] *Alone*—As he is the whole universe and there is nothing other than he.

न कदाचिज्जगत्यस्मिन् तत्त्वज्ञो हन्त खिद्यति ।
यत एकेन तेनेदं पूर्णं ब्रह्माण्डमण्डलम् ॥ २ ॥

हन्त Oh अस्मिन् this जगति in world तत्त्वज्ञ: knower of Truth कदाचित् ever न not खिद्यति feels misery यत: for एकेन alone तेन by himself इदं this ब्रह्माण्डमण्डलम् whole universe पूर्णं filled.

2. Oh, the knower[1] of Truth is never miserable in this world, for the whole universe is filled by himself alone.

[1] *Knower etc.*—The sense of misery is possible only with the perception of duality. He who perceives nothing but himself in the whole universe cannot be touched by sorrow.

न जातु विषयाः केऽपि स्वारामं हर्षयन्त्यमी ।
सल्लकीपल्लवप्रीतिमिवेभं निम्बपल्लवाः ॥ ३ ॥

सल्लकीपल्लवप्रीतम् Who delights in sallaki leaves इभं elephant निम्बपल्लवा: leaves of the neem tree इव as अमी those के अपि any विषयाः objects स्वारामं one delighting in Self जातु at any time न not हर्षयन्ति please.

3. No[1] sense-objects ever please him who delights in the Self, even as the leaves of the neem tree do not please an elephant who delights in sallaki leaves.

[1] *No etc.*—The objects of the senses lose all their charm for one who has realized the ultimate perennial source of absolute bliss in the Self and the nothingness of sense-objects.

यस्तु भोगेषु भुक्तेषु न भवत्यधिवासितः ।
अभुक्तेषु निराकाङ्क्षी तादृशो भवदुर्लभः ॥ ४ ॥

य: Who तु (expletive) भुक्तेषु experienced भोगेषु in

objects of enjoyment अधिवासित: on whom impressions are left न not भवति is अमुक्तेषु in things not enjoyed (च and) निराकाङ्क्षी having no desire ताद्दश: such a one भवदुर्लभ: rare in the world.

4. Rare in this world is he[1] on whom impressions are not left of things which he has experienced or who does not desire things which he has not yet experienced.

[1] *He etc.*—A man of true knowledge perceives nothing but himself in the universe. He has therefore nothing else with which to identify himself. He is free from the sense of 'I' and 'mine'. All his actions therefore are but apparent and do not leave any impress on his mind. He is not attached to the objects of the world, nor do they have any attraction for him.

बुभुक्षुरिह संसारे मुमुक्षुरपि द्दश्यते ।
भोगमोक्षनिराकाङ्क्षी विरलो हि महाशयः ॥ ५ ॥

इह Here संसारे in the world बुभुक्षु: one who desires worldly enjoyments मुमुक्षु: one who desires liberation अपि also द्दश्यते is seen भोगमोक्षनिराकाङ्क्षी not desirous of enjoyment or liberation महाशय: the great-souled one हि indeed विरल: rare.

5. Those desirous of worldly enjoyment and those desirous of liberation, both are found in this world. But rare indeed is the great-souled one who[1] is not desirous of either enjoyment or liberation.

[1] *Who etc.*—Even the desire for liberation is an imperfection, for it implies the consciousness of bondage. Absolute Knowledge transcends the consciousness of both enjoyment and liberation.

धर्मार्थकाममोक्षेषु जीविते मरणे तथा ।
कस्याप्युदारचित्तस्य हेयोपादेयता न हि ॥ ६ ॥

कस्य अपि Rare उदारचित्तस्य of a broad-minded person हि indeed धर्मार्थकाममोक्षेषु in *dharma, artha, kāma,* and *mokṣa* तथा as well as जीविते in life मरणे in death हेयोपादेयता attraction or aversion न not (अस्ति is).

6. Rare is the broad-minded person who has neither attraction for, nor aversion to, *dharma* (duty), *artha* (worldly prosperity), *kāma* (desire), and *mokṣa* (liberation) as well as life[1] and death.

[1] *Life etc.*—A man of Self-knowledge is ever conscious of himself as eternal. He has no body-idea. Life and death are meaningless to him.

वाञ्छा न विश्वविलये न द्वेषस्तस्य च स्थितौ ।
यथा जीविकया तस्माद्धन्य आस्ते यथासुखम् ॥ ७ ॥

(ज्ञानिनः Of a man of Knowledge) विश्वविलये in the dissolution of the universe वाञ्छा desire न not तस्य its स्थितौ in existence च and द्वेषः aversion न not (अस्ति is) तस्मात् so धन्यः the blessed one यथा जीविकया with whatever living comes of itself यथासुखम् happily आस्ते lives.

7. The man of Knowledge does[1] not feel any desire for the dissolution of the universe, or aversion to its existence. The blessed one, therefore, lives happily on whatever[2] subsistence comes as a matter of course.

[1] *Does etc.*—Because he perceives the universe as the Self itself. As long as there is ignorance, one looks upon

the world as the root of all misery and tries to shun or
destroy it, so to speak. But with the birth of Knowledge
of the Self, his vision is changed and everything is revealed
as the Self alone.

   [2] *Whatever etc.*—Because he does not make any effort
for his subsistence, owing to his ego having been completely annihilated.

कृतार्थोऽनेन ज्ञानेनेत्येवं गलितधीः कृती ।

पश्यन् शृण्वन् स्पृशन् जिघ्रन्नश्नास्ते यथासुखम् ॥ ८ ॥

अनेन This ज्ञानेन by Knowledge कृतार्थः fulfilled इति
एवं thus गलितधीः with the mind absorbed कृती contented
पश्यन् seeing शृण्वन् hearing स्पृशन् touching जिघ्रन् smelling
अश्नन् eating यथासुखम् happily आस्ते lives.

   8. Being fulfilled by the knowledge of the Self
and with his mind absorbed,[1] and contented,[2] the
wise one lives happily, seeing,[3] hearing, touching,
smelling, and eating.

   [1] *Absorbed.*—immersed in the glory of Self-knowledge
and its resultant blessings.

   [2] *Contented*—Because nothing remains to be attained.

   [3] *Seeing etc.*—It is not external behaviour, but internal
consciousness that differentiates a man of Knowledge
from an ordinary human being. Externally, they may
have everything in common. But internally the man of
Knowledge is ever free and never identifies himself with
the objects of the senses; whereas an ignorant man always
does so, and thus remains bound.

शून्या दृष्टिर्वृथा चेष्टा विकलानीन्द्रियाणि च ।

न स्पृहा न विरक्तिर्वा क्षीणसंसारसागरे ॥ ९ ॥

क्षीणसंसारसागरे In one for whom the ocean of the

world has dried up स्पृहा attachment न not विरक्ति: aversion वा or न not (अस्ति is तस्य his) दृष्टि: look शून्या vacant चेष्टा action वृथा purposeless इन्द्रयाणि senses (च and) विकलानि inoperative.

9. There is no attachment or aversion in one for whom the ocean[1] of the world has dried[2] up. His look is vacant,[3] his action purposeless,[4] and his senses inoperative.[5]

[1] *Ocean etc.*—The world (life of birth and rebirth) is likened to an ocean. He who falls into an ocean is buffeted about and carried hither and thither by the waves; he finds it hard to reach the shore and there is untold suffering. In *saṁsāra*, the ocean of the world, *karmas* and desires move us hither and thither, we suffer greatly and cannot reach the goal of Self-knowledge.

[2] *Dried etc.*—When one realizes the Self, one is free from ignorance and its resultant *karmas* and desires.

[3] *Vacant*—Because he has no inner motive whatsoever.

[4] *Purposeless*—Because his actions have no end in view.

[5] *Inoperative*—Because the objects of the senses do not leave any impressions on his mind.

न जागर्ति न निद्राति नोन्मीलति न मीलति ।

अहो परदशा कापि वर्तते मुक्तचेतसः ॥ १० ॥

(ज्ञानी The wise one) न not जागर्ति keeps awake न not निद्राति sleeps न not उन्मीलति opens eyes न not मीलति closes eyes अहो Oh मुक्तचेतस: of a liberated soul क्व अपि anywhere परदशा supreme condition वर्तते is.

10. The wise one neither[1] keeps awake nor sleeps, he neither opens nor closes his eyes. Oh, the

liberated soul anywhere[2] enjoys the supreme condition.

[1] *Neither etc.*—A liberated soul may not be called awake as he does not seek the objects of the world, nor does he perceive them as we do. He is dead to the relative world. He may not be called sleeping either, as he is ever conscious of the Self pervading the universe.

[2] *Anywhere*—under all circumstances.

सर्वत्र दृश्यते स्वस्थः सर्वत्र विमलाशयः ।
समस्तवासनामुक्तो मुक्तः सर्वत्र राजते ॥ ११ ॥

मुक्तः The liberated person सर्वत्र always स्वस्थः abiding in the Self सर्वत्र always विमलाशयः pure in heart दृश्यते is seen सर्वत्र under all conditions समस्तवासनामुक्तः freed from all desires (सन् being) राजते lives.

11. The liberated one is always found abiding in the Self and is pure[1] in heart; he lives freed from all desires, under all conditions.

[1] *Pure etc.*—not attached to any worldly object.

पश्यन् श्रृण्वन् स्पृशन् जिघ्रन्नश्नन् गृह्लन् वदन् व्रजन् ।
ईहितानीहितैर्मुक्तो मुक्त एव महाशयः ॥ १२ ॥

पश्यन् Seeing श्रृण्वन् hearing स्पृशन् touching जिघ्रन् smelling अश्नन् eating गृह्लन् taking वदन् speaking व्रजन् walking ईहितानीहितैः frcm efforts and non-efforts मुक्तः free महाशयः man of great soul मुक्तः free एव indeed.

12. Seeing, hearing, touching, smelling, eating, taking, speaking, and walking, the great-souled one,

free from all efforts and non-efforts, is verily emancipated.

True knowledge does not necessarily lie in the
cessation of action but in the absence of attachment.
The knower of the Self, therefore, even if he acts, does
not in reality act. He is ever free, though his behaviour
may seem the same as that of others. He is above action
and inaction.

न निन्दति न च स्तौति न हृष्यति न कुप्यति ।

न ददाति न गृह्णाति मुक्तः सर्वत्र नीरसः ॥ १३ ॥

मुक्तः The liberated one न not निन्दति slanders न not
स्तौति praises न not हृष्यति rejoices न not कुप्यति is angry
न not ददाति gives न not गृह्णाति takes च and (सः he)
सर्वत्र in all objects नीरसः free from attachment.

13. The liberated one neither slanders nor
praises, he neither rejoices nor is he angry, he neither
gives nor takes. He is free from attachment to all
objects.

सानुरागां स्त्रियं दृष्ट्वा मृत्युं वा समुपस्थितम् ।

अविह्वलमनाः स्वस्थो मुक्त एव महाशयः ॥ १४ ॥

सानुरागां Loving स्त्रियं woman समुपस्थितम् near at
hand मृत्युं death वा or दृष्ट्वा seeing महाशयः the great-souled
one अविह्वलमनाः unperturbed in mind स्वस्थः self-poised
(तिष्ठति remains सः he) मुक्तः emancipated एव indeed.

14. The great-souled one is not perturbed and
remains self-poised at[1] the sight of a woman full of
love as well as of approaching death. He is indeed[2]
liberated.

¹ *At etc.*—Two opposite cases are cited—the most pleasant and the most terrible. The liberated one remains the same under both these conditions.

² *Indeed etc.*—Such equanimity is a true sign of liberation.

सुखे दुःखे नरे नार्यां सम्पत्सु च विपत्सु च ।
विशेषो नैव धीरस्य सर्वत्रसमदर्शिनः ॥ १५ ॥

सर्वत्र Everywhere समदर्शिनः seeing the same धीरस्य of the steady one सुखे in happiness दुःखे in misery नरे in man नार्यां in woman सम्पत्सु in prosperity च (expletive) विपत्सु in adversity च and विशेषः difference न not एव verily (भवति is).

15. The steady one who sees the same everywhere, sees no difference between happiness and misery, man and woman, and prosperity and adversity.

न हिंसा नैव कारुण्यं नौद्धत्यं न च दीनता ।
नाश्चर्यं नैव च क्षोभः क्षीणसंसरणेऽनरे ॥ १६ ॥

क्षीणसंसरणे Whose worldly life is exhausted अनरे who has transcended the limitations of human nature (विदुषि in the wise one) कारुण्यं mercy न not हिंसा desire to harm न not एव surely दीनता humility न not औद्धत्यं insolence च and न not आश्चर्यं wonder न not क्षोभः mental disturbance च and न not एव surely (भवति are).

16. In the wise one whose worldly¹ life is exhausted and who has transcended the limitations of human nature, there is neither² compassion nor

any desire to harm, neither humility nor insolence,
neither wonder nor mental disturbance.

[1] *Worldly etc.*—He is no longer bound by ignorance
which causes the rounds of birth and death. He is illumined and has destroyed the bondages of desire and
Karma.

[2] *Neither etc.*—These opposites do not exist in him.
He is above them.

न मुक्तो विषयद्वेष्टा न वा विषयलोलुपः ।

असंसक्तमना नित्यं प्राप्तं प्राप्तमुपाश्नुते ॥ १७ ॥

मुक्तः The liberated one विषयद्वेष्टा abhorrent of the
objects of the senses न not विषयलोलुपः craving for the
objects of the senses न not वा or (सः he) नित्यं ever
असंसक्तमनाः with a detached mind प्राप्तं coming as a matter of course प्राप्तम् sense-objects उपाश्नुते enjoys.

17. The liberated one neither[1] abhors the objects of the senses nor craves for them. Ever with a
detached mind he experiences them as they come.

[1] *Neither etc.*—Because abhorrence and craving are
both due to attachment, from which a liberated soul is
ever free.

समाधानासमाधानहिताहितविकल्पनाः ।

शून्यचित्तो न जानाति कैवल्यमिव संस्थितः ॥ १८ ॥

शून्यचित्तः Of vacant mind (ज्ञानी wise one) समाधाना-
समाधानहिताहितविकल्पनाः the alternatives of contemplation and non-contemplation, good and evil न not जानाति
knows (सः he) कैवल्यम् in the state of Absoluteness संस्थितः
abiding इव as it were.

18. The wise one of vacant[1] mind knows[2] not the conflict of contemplation and non-contemplation, good and evil. He abides as it were in the state of Absoluteness.

[1] *Vacant*—unattached to the world. No desire arises in his mind. It is filled with the consciousness of the Self alone.

[2] *Knows etc.*—Because all such conflicts arise only in connection with the consciousness of relative life, which he has transcended.

निर्ममो निरहङ्कारो न किञ्चिदिति निश्चितः ।
अन्तर्गलितसर्वाशः कुर्वन्नपि करोति न ॥ १९ ॥

(ज्ञानी The man of Knowledge) निर्मम: devoid of the feeling of 'mine' निरहङ्कार: devoid of the feeling of 'I' किञ्चित् anything न not (अस्ति is) इति this निश्चित: knowing for certain अन्तर्गलितसर्वाश: with all desires gone from within (सन् being) कुर्वन् doing अपि though न not करोति does.

19. Devoid of the feeling of 'I' and 'mine', knowing for certain that nothing is, and with all his inner desires set at rest, the man of Knowledge does[1] not act though he may be acting.

[1] *Does etc.*—Action, as we ordinarily understand it, presupposes the sense of egoism on the part of the doer. A man of Knowledge, however, transcends this sense of egoism. All his actions, therefore, though apparently the same as those of ordinary people, are not essentially on a par with them. His actions do not produce any binding effects, while those of others entail new and fresh bondages.

मनःप्रकाशसम्मोहस्वप्नजाड्यविवर्जितः ।
दशां कामपि संप्राप्तो भवेद्गलितमानसः ॥ २० ॥

गलितमानसः Whose mind has melted away मनःप्रकाश-
सम्मोहस्वप्नजाड्यविवर्जितः the functions of whose mind have
ceased to operate and who is free from delusion, dreaming, and dullness (ज्ञानी wise one) काम् अपि indescribable दशां condition संप्राप्तः भवेत् attains.

20. An indescribable state is attained by the
wise one whose mind has melted away, its functions
having ceased to operate, and who is free from
delusion, dreaming, and dullness.

A man of Self-knowledge has his mind completely
purged of all delusion, inertia, etc., that obstruct the
vision of the Reality. In such a state, all the functions of
the mind, *vrttis*, cease to operate, and it is as good as
destroyed. Then the final realization bursts forth, of which
no description is ever possible.

CHAPTER XVIII

PEACE

अष्टावक्र उवाच ।

यस्य बोधोदये तावत् स्वप्नवद्भवति भ्रमः ।
तस्मै सुखैकरूपाय नमः शान्ताय तेजसे ॥ १ ॥

अष्टावक्रः Aṣṭāvakra उवाच said:

यस्य Of which बोधोदये with the dawning of knowledge तावत् all भ्रमः delusion स्वप्नवत् like dream भवति becomes सुखैकरूपाय which is Bliss itself by nature शान्ताय calm तेजसे effulgence तस्मै to That नमः salutation.

Aṣṭāvakra said:

1. Salutation to That which is Bliss itself by nature, calmness,[1] and effulgence,[2] with[3] the dawning of the knowledge of which all delusion[4] becomes like a dream.

[1] *Calmness*—the Transcendental in which there is no change.

[2] *Effulgence*—The Ātman is self-effulgent: nothing else can perceive It. Though unknowable, it is known to Itself by Itself.

[3] *With etc.*—The world which now appears so real to us changes its nature with the realization of the Self, and appears unreal as a dream. It then loses all its charms and attractions as well as its terrors, just as the alluring visions of a dream, or the terrors of a nightmare, fade on waking.

⁴ *Delusion*—the phenomenal universe which is illusory.

अर्जयित्वाऽखिलानर्थान् भोगानाप्नोति पुष्कलान् ।
न हि सर्वपरित्यागमन्तरेण सुखी भवेत् ॥ २ ॥

(कश्चित् One) अखिलान् all अर्थान् worldly objects अर्जयित्वा acquiring पुष्कलान् abundant भोगान् enjoyments आप्नोति attains सर्वपरित्यागमन्तरेण without the renunciation of all हि surely सुखी happy न not भवेत् becomes.

2. One gets plenty of enjoyments by acquiring all kinds of worldly objects. Surely[1] one cannot be happy without renouncing all.

[1] *Surely etc.*—That renunciation alone removes all fear and makes us truly happy is very beautifully illustrated by Bhartṛhari in a verse in his *A Hundred Verses on Renunciation*. He says: 'In enjoyment, there is the fear of disease; in social position, the fear of a fall; in wealth, the fear of (hostile) kings; in honour, the fear of humiliation; in power, the fear of foes; in beauty, the fear of old age; in scriptural erudition, the fear of opponents; in virtue, the fear of seducers; in the body, the fear of death. All the things of the world pertaining to men are attended with fear; renunciation alone eliminates all fear.'

Sense-enjoyment and true happiness do not go together. They are contradictory.

कर्तव्यदुःखमार्तण्डज्वालादग्धान्तरात्मनः ।
कुतः प्रशमपीयूषधारासारमृते सुखम् ॥ ३ ॥

कर्तव्यदुःखमार्तण्डज्वालादग्धान्तरात्मनः Of one whose heart's core has been scorched by the heat of the sun of the sorrow of duty प्रशमपीयूषधारासारम् ऋते without the

torrential shower of the ambrosia of tranquillity कुतः
how सुखम् happiness (स्यात् is).

3. How can one whose[1] heart's core has been
scorched by the heat of the sun of sorrow arising
from duty enjoy happiness without the continuous
shower of the ambrosia of tranquillity?[2]

[1] *Whose etc.*—Duty, as it is ordinarily understood, is
nothing but slavery in the form of virtue. It is the morbid
attachment of flesh for flesh, the absurd greed for gold
and gain or other worldly things to which we feel attached. Only those who consider the world real find that they
have things to do, duties to fulfil. The sense of duty,
therefore, arises ultimately from ignorance. And it
binds us to the relative life, subjecting us to all the miseries
of the world. This scorches our innermost soul.

[2] *Tranquillity*—When the *vṛttis* of the mind have sub-
sided, when the mind has been freed of desires, then the
relative life loses its grip. We feel that the world is ephem-
eral and we have nothing to do in or with it. *Then* comes
calmness which is real happiness. This calmness is like
ambrosia poured forth like rain to revive the parched-up
heart.

भवोऽयं भावनामात्रो न किञ्चित् परमार्थतः ।

नास्त्यभावः स्वभावानां भावाभावविभाविनाम् ॥ ४ ॥

अयं This भवः universe भावनामात्रः mere thought
परमार्थतः in reality किञ्चित् anything न not भावाभावविभा-
विनाम् inherent in the existent and the non-existent स्वभा-
वानां of nature अभावः non-existence न not अस्ति is.

4. This universe is but a state[1] of consciousness.
In reality it is nothing. The existent[2] and the non-
existent[3] do[4] not lose their inherent nature.

[1] *State etc.*—The universe has no existence independent of the Self. What we see is only the projection of the mind. The moment we bring about a change in our consciousness, the universe changes for us.

[2] *Existent*—the Self.

[3] *Non-existent*—the universe.

[4] *Do etc.*—The Self does not lose its own nature which is Existence itself; nor does the universe lose its own nature which is unreality or non-existence.

The implication of the verse is this: The Self is the only real substance. Existence is its very nature. The Self therefore can never be non-existent, as nothing can lose its own nature. Likewise, the universe is unreal. It is superimposed on the Self as a snake is superimposed on a rope. It has no existence independent of the Self. Non-existence is its very nature.

न दूरं न च सङ्कोचाल्लब्धमेवात्मनः पदम् ।
निर्विकल्पं निरायासं निर्विकारं निरञ्जनम् ॥ ५ ॥

निर्विकल्पं Absolute निरायासं effortless निर्विकारं immutable निरञ्जनम् spotless आत्मनः पदम् the nature of the Self न not दूरं far न not च and सङ्कोचात् limited (वर्तते is) लब्धम् attained एव verily.

5. The Self which is absolute, effortless[1], immutable, and spotless[2] is neither[3] far away nor limited. It[4] is verily ever attained.

[1] *Effortless*—Being one without a second, the Self has nothing to exert for. It is ever inactive—calm and serene.

[2] *Spotless*—beyond all attributes.

[3] *Neither etc.*—The Self is all-pervasive, One, and is therefore neither far nor near. It is not limited.

[4] *It etc.*—unlike sense-objects, which are attainable

because they are limited and different from us. The Self is our very nature and so it cannot be attained. It is ever attained.

व्यामोहमात्रविरतौ स्वरूपादानमात्रतः ।
वीतशोका विराजन्ते निरावरणदृष्टयः ॥ ६ ॥

निरावरणदृष्टयः Those whose vision is unveiled व्यामोह-मात्रविरतौ as soon as illusion ceases स्वरूपादानमात्रतः as soon as the Self is realized वीतशोकाः with sorrows dispelled विराजन्ते exist.

6. Those whose vision is unveiled as soon as illusion ceases and the Self is realized, live with their sorrows dispelled.

समस्तं कल्पनामात्रमात्मा मुक्तः सनातनः ।
इति विज्ञाय धीरो हि किमभ्यस्यति बालवत् ॥ ७ ॥

समस्तं All कल्पनामात्रम् mere imagination आत्मा Self मुक्तः free सनातनः eternal इति this विज्ञाय knowing धीरः the wise one हि indeed किम् (interrogative) बालवत् like a child अभ्यस्यति acts.

7. Knowing all as mere imagination and the Self as free and eternal, does the wise one act ignorantly like a child?

आत्मा ब्रह्मेति निश्चित्य भावाभावौ च कल्पितौ ।
निष्कामः किं विजानाति किं ब्रूते च करोति किम् ॥ ८ ॥

आत्मा Self ब्रह्म Brahman भावाभावौ existence and non-existence च and कल्पितौ imagined इति this निश्चित्य

knowing for certain निष्काम: one who is free from
desire किं what विजानाति knows किं what ब्रूते says किम्
what च and करोति does.

8. Knowing for certain that one's self is Brahman and that existence[1] and non-existence are
figments, what[2] does one who is free from desire,
know, say, or do?

[1] *Existence etc.*—Relative existence and absolute non-
existence are both mental projections. Both of them are
figments. Relative existence is apparent. Relatively existent objects vanish with the knowledge of the Absolute
Reality, just as the world vanishes with the knowledge
of the Self. Absolute non-existence is merely imaginary.
Absolutely non-existent objects, such as a flower in the
sky or the child of a barren woman, do not exist even
apparently. Both relative existence and absolute non-
existence, however, have their basis in Absolute Existence,
the Self.

[2] *What etc.*—To one who has attained Self-knowledge
nothing else remains to be known. He becomes fulfilled,
free from desire. Worldly things appear to him contemptible, having neither reality nor unreality. Bereft of
egoism as he becomes, he knows not, speaks not, and
acts not, though apparently he may be doing all these.

अयं सोऽहमयं नाहमिति क्षीणा विकल्पनाः ।
सर्वमात्मेति निश्चित्य तूष्णीम्भूतस्य योगिनः ॥ ९ ॥

सर्वम् All आत्मा Self इति this निश्चित्य knowing for
certain तूष्णीम्भूतस्य become silent योगिनः of the *yogin* अयं
सः this indeed अहम् I अयं this अहं I न not इति such
विकल्पनाः thoughts क्षीणाः annihilated (भवन्ति become).

9. Such thoughts[1] as 'this indeed am I' and

'this I am not' are annihilated for the *yogin* who has become silent by knowing for certain all as the Self.

¹ *Thoughts etc.*—With the dawn of Self-knowledge —when all is revealed as the Self and nothing but the Self—all dual conceptions vanish. The *yogin* then realizes that he is all.

न विक्षेपो न चैकाग्रयं नातिबोधो न मूढता ।
न सुखं न च वा दुःखमुपशान्तस्य योगिनः ॥ १० ॥

उपशान्तस्य Who has become tranquil योगिनः of the *yogin* विक्षेपः distraction न not ऐकाग्रयं concentration च and न not अतिबोधः increase of knowledge न not मूढता ignorance न not सुखं pleasure न not दुःखम् pain वा or न not च (expletive) (भवति is).

10. The *yogin* who has attained tranquillity, has no¹ distraction, no concentration, no increase in knowledge, no ignorance, and neither pleasure nor pain.

¹ *No etc.*—A *yogin* with control over his senses has his mind perfectly balanced and tranquil. No distraction whatsoever, therefore, can affect his equanimity. He has perfect poise.

स्वाराज्ये भैक्ष्यवृत्तौ च लाभालाभे जने वने ।
निर्विकल्पस्वभावस्य न विशेषोऽस्ति योगिनः ॥ ११ ॥

निर्विकल्पस्वभावस्य Whose nature is unconditioned योगिनः of the *yogin* स्वाराज्ये in the dominion of heaven भैक्ष्यवृत्तौ in mendicancy लाभालाभे in gain or loss जने in

society वने in forest च and विशेष: difference न not अस्ति
is.

11. In heaven[1] or in beggary, in gain or loss,
in society or solitude, there is no difference to the
unconditioned *yogin*.

[1] *Heaven etc.*—To feel different under these different
conditions is possible only for one whose mind is conditioned, bound, and limited by relative consciousness.
When one has transcended that state of consciousness,
extremes of fortune make no difference. They appear
unsubstantial, shadowy.

क्व धर्मः क्व च वा कामः क्व चार्थः क्व विवेकिता ।
इदं कृतमिदं नेति द्वन्द्वैर्मुक्तस्य योगिनः ॥ १२ ॥

इदं This कृतम् done इदं this न not (कृतम् done)
इति this द्वन्द्वै: from the pairs of opposites मुक्तस्य free योगिन:
of the *yogin* क्व where धर्म: *dharma* क्व where अर्थ: *artha* क्व
where च and काम: *kāma* क्व where वा or विवेकिता discrimination.

12. Where is *dharma* (performance of ritualistic
or meritorious works), where is *artha* (worldly prosperity), where is *kāma* (sense-enjoyment), and
where is discrimination for the *yogin* who has transcended such dual notions as 'this is to be done'
and 'this is not to be done'?

The idea is this: The sense of 'to be done' and 'not
to be done', which are typical of the pairs of opposites,
springs from relative consciousness, from ignorance and
and desire. We are always active under the impulse of
desire, securing some objects of desire, and still seeking
others. This desire is at the root of all *dharma, artha,* and

kāma and also of discrimination—for were we not blinded and bound by ignorance and desire, there would be no necessity for us to discriminate the real from the unreal; the unreal would simply not exist for us. One free from the pairs of opposites has, therefore, no use for *dharma*, *artha*, and *kāma*.

कृत्यं किमपि नैवास्ति न कापि हृदि रञ्जना ।
यथाजीवनमेवेह जीवन्मुक्तस्य योगिनः ॥ १३ ॥

जीवन्मुक्तस्य Liberated while living योगिनः of the *yogin* किम् अपि any कृत्यं duty न not एव surely अस्ति is हृदि at heart का अपि any रञ्जना attachment न not (अस्ति is अस्य कृत्यम् his action) इह in this world यथाजीवनम् pertaining to life एव only (भवति is).

13. The *yogin* who is liberated[1] while living, has neither[2] any duty nor any attachment at heart. His actions[3] pertain to the present life only, being merely the effects of his past *karma*.

[1] *Liberated etc.*—The *jivanmukta* is one whose ignorance, with all its modifications, has been completely eradicated and who, rid of all bondage, abides in the Absolute Self. His is a state in which 'the knots of his heart are torn asunder, all his doubts are removed, and the effects of his actions are destroyed by the realization of the Supreme One'. The *Upadeśasāhasrī* of Sankarā-cārya describes his state thus: 'The knower of the Self is indeed he, and no other, who does not see in the waking state, being as if he were asleep; who, being One without a second, does not perceive duality, even though he may see objects; and who is inactive even though he may perform actions.'

[2] *Neither etc.*—Because with the attainment of liberation, the *yogin* gets rid of the dual notions of 'I' and 'mine'

and consequently, along with them, the attachment and
sense of duty that spring from them. Not that all physical
actions necessarily cease for a liberated soul, but they
are no longer impelled by the feeling of egoism.

³ *Actions etc.*—A very important fact in the life of the
liberated soul is mentioned in this verse. So long as the
liberated one lives, he is found to act. Yet he is said to be
inactive. This apparent contradiction is explained here.
The *yogin* is internally free. He does not feel any desire
for anything, or the need to do anything. But the very
fact that his body still exists shows that there is some
force holding the body. This is the *prārabdha karma* of the
yogin. This *karma* continues to operate, but the *yogin* is not
affected. His bodily actions and also actions in the surface
mind go on until the *prārabdha karma* is worked out. Then
the body drops off, and there is absolute emancipation
for the *yogin*. From this standpoint, the man of Realization has neither a body, being beyond body idea, nor
prārabdha. These are merely our explanation, for we, in
our ignorance, see him as having a body and as being
active. That is why the *yogin's* actions have been called
yathājīvanam, pertaining to the present life only.

क मोहः क च वा विश्वं क तद्धानं क मुक्तता ।
सर्वसङ्कल्पसीमायां विश्रान्तस्य महात्मनः ॥ १४ ॥

सर्वसङ्कल्पसीमायां Beyond the border of the world of
desires विश्रान्तस्य resting महात्मनः of the great-souled one
मोहः delusion क where च (expletive) विश्वं universe क
where तद्धानं its renunciation क where मुक्तता liberation
क where वा or.

14. Where is delusion, where is the universe,
where is renunciation, moreover where is liberation
for the great-souled one who rests beyond[1] the world
of desires?

[1] *Beyond etc.*—Truly speaking, existence is one. It is only desire that demarcates it and creates the illusion of the relative world and along with it the necessity of getting out of it. The moment one is freed from desire, the illusion of the universe with all its consequences vanishes.

येन विश्वमिदं दृष्टं स नास्तीति करोतु वै ।
निर्वासनः किं कुरुते पश्यन्नपि न पश्यति ॥ १५ ॥

येन By whom इदं this विश्वम् universe दृष्टं is seen सः he (विश्व universe) न not अस्ति is इति this करोतु may do वै (expletive) निर्वासनः one who is desireless किं what कुरुते has to do (सः he) पश्यन् seeing अपि though न not पश्यति sees.

15. He[1] who sees the universe may try to deny it. What has the desireless to do? He sees[2] not even though he sees.

[1] *He etc.*—Really the universe is not as we see it and feel it, which we do in ignorance under the sway of desire. One who is aware of the phenomenal world must try to negate it, for he is still in ignorance. One who is beyond ignorance and desire has nothing to do with it.

[2] *Sees etc.*—To a man of Realization the universe appears unsubstantial and illusory. He cannot, therefore, be said to be seeing the universe as we understand it, as something real and substantial.

येन दृष्टं परं ब्रह्म सोऽहं ब्रह्म ति चिन्तयेत् ।
किं चिन्तयति निश्चिन्तो द्वितीयं यो न पश्यति ॥ १६ ॥

येन By whom परं supreme ब्रह्म Brahman दृष्टं is seen सः he अहं ब्रह्म I am Brahman इति this चिन्तयेत् thinks

य: who द्वितीयं second न not पश्यति sees (स: that) निश्चिन्त:
one who has transcended thought किं what चिन्तयति
thinks.

16. He[1] who has seen the Supreme Brahman
meditates, 'I am Brahman'. What does he who has
transcended all thought think, when he sees no
second?

[1] *He etc.*—A very subtle distinction is made here. He
who *sees* Brahman has evidently not reached the highest
state and realized his identity with Brahman. The dual
consciousness—I and Brahman—is still there, making it
possible for him to meditate, 'I am Brahman'. But when
the highest state is reached, identity is established, the
dual consciousness is totally destroyed, and no such
meditation is possible or needed.

दृष्टो येनात्मविक्षेपो निरोधं कुरुते त्वसौ ।
उदारस्तु न विक्षिप्त: साध्याभावात्करोति किम् ॥ १७ ॥

येन By whom आत्मविक्षेप: distraction in self दृष्ट: is
seen असौ he तु indeed निरोधं कुरुते practises control उदार:
the noble-minded one तु but विक्षिप्त: distracted न not
(भवति is स: he) साध्याभावात् having nothing to accomplish किम् what करोति does.

17. He, indeed, controls[1] himself who sees
distraction in himself. But the great[2] one is not distracted. Having nothing to accomplish,[3] what does
he do?

[1] *Controls etc.*—Distraction, outward or inward, in
any form, is caused only by the identification of the Self
with the non-self, which is due to ignorance. It has,
therefore, no place in the man of Self-knowledge. Con-
trolling the mind is meaningless to him.

11

² *Great etc.*—One who perceives the Self as One without a second.

³ *Accomplish*—by way of getting rid of duality and its concomitant distractions.

धीरो लोकविपर्यस्तो वर्तमानोऽपि लोकवत् ।
न समाधिं न विक्षेपं न लेपं स्वस्य पश्यति ॥ १८ ॥

लोकवत् Like an ordinary man वर्तमान: existing अपि though धीर: the man of Knowledge लोकविपर्यस्त: contrary to the ordinary man (स: he) स्वस्य of his own समाधिं concentration न not विक्षेपं distraction न not लेपं stain न not पश्यति sees.

18. The man of Knowledge, though[1] living like an ordinary man, is contrary to him. He sees[2] neither concentration nor distraction nor defilement of his own.

¹ *Though etc.*—The external behaviour of the man of Knowledge seems like that of other people, but there is a fundamental difference between his outlook and theirs. Ordinary people look upon the world as real and substantial, and behave accordingly; but the man of Knowledge knows and feels it to be illusory and unsubstantial, and his behaviour in it is only apparent. His actions are no longer voluntary but are impelled only by the momentum of the effects of those actions that are responsible for his life in this world. His body drops off as soon as those effects are exhausted.

² *Sees etc.*—For he sees nothing but the Self which is Pure Intelligence.

भावाभावविहीनो यस्तृप्तो निर्वासनो बुध: ।
नैव किञ्चित् कृतं तेन लोकदृष्ट्या विकुर्वता ॥ १९ ॥

य: Who भावाभावविहीन: devoid of existence and non-existence तृप्त: satisfied निर्वासन: free from desire बुध: wise लोकदृष्ट्या in the sight of the world विकुर्वता acting तेन by him किञ्चित् anything एव even न not कृतं done.

19. He who is beyond[1] existence and non-existence, who is wise, satisfied, and free from desire, does[2] nothing even if he may be acting in the eyes of the world.

[1] *Beyond etc.*—beyond the relative world which is a mixture of existence and non-existence. The world is said to be existent as it is perceived in ordinary consciousness, but to be non-existent as it is lost in superconsciousness. Knowing the nature of the world, the man of Knowledge is quite unconcerned with it.

[2] *Does etc.*—Actions are no longer actions when they are not accompanied by the feeling of egoism. The man of Knowledge is absolutely free from it. He does not identify himself with his actions. He is, therefore, really inactive, even though he may seem to be acting.

प्रवृत्तौ वा निवृत्तौ वा नैव धीरस्य दुर्ग्रहः ।
यदा यत्कर्तुमायाति तत्कृत्वा तिष्ठतः सुखम् ॥ २० ॥

यदा When यत् what कर्तुम् to do आयाति comes तत् that कृत्वा doing सुखम् happily तिष्ठत: living धीरस्य of the wise one प्रवृत्तौ in activity वा (expletive) निवृत्तौ in inactivity वा or दुर्ग्रहः uneasiness न not एव surely (अस्ति is).

20. The wise one who lives on happily doing what[1] comes to him to be done, does[2] not feel eagerness either in activity or in inactivity.

[1] *What etc.*—as a matter of course on account of *prārabdha*.

² *Does etc.*—Because he no longer engages himself in
any action, nor does he refrain from any action, out of
his own will. Voluntary actions breed unhappiness when
they are frustrated or impeded. Devoid of the feeling of
egoism, he is the same in activity and inactivity.

निर्वासनो निरालम्बः स्वच्छन्दो मुक्तबन्धनः ।

क्षिप्तः संस्कारवातेन चेष्टते शुष्कपर्णवत् ॥ २१ ॥

निर्वासनः Desireless निरालम्बः independent स्वच्छन्दः
free मुक्तबन्धनः free from bondage (जनः man) संस्कारवातेन
by the wind of the effects of past actions क्षिप्तः cast
(सन् being) शुष्कपर्णवत् like a dry leaf चेष्टते moves.

21. Blown by the wind of the *saṃskāras*, the
desireless, independent, free, and liberated person
moves[1] about like a dry leaf.

¹ *Moves etc.*—Just as a dry leaf is blown about by the
wind, hither and thither, not of its own choosing, so the
man of Knowledge is guided by his *prārabdha* without the
least vestige of egoism in him.

असंसारस्य तु क्वापि न हर्षो न विषादता ।

स शीतलमना नित्यं विदेह इव राजते ॥ २२ ॥

असंसारस्य Of one who has transcended worldly
existence तु (expletive) क्व अपि anywhere हर्षः joy न not
विषादता sorrow न not (अस्ति is) नित्यं ever शीतलमनाः
cool-minded सः he विदेहः one without a body इव as
if राजते exists.

22. There is no[1] joy or sorrow for one who has
transcended worldly existence. Ever with a serene[2]
mind, he lives like one without a body.

[1] *No etc.*—Joy and sorrow are different modifications of the uncontrolled mind and originate from desire for relative things, which is at the root of worldly existence. Therefore one who has transcended worldly existence has gone beyond both joy and sorrow.

[2] *Serene*—devoid of any distractions whatsoever.

कुत्रापि न जिहासास्ति नाशो वापि न कुत्रचित् ।
आत्मारामस्य धीरस्य शीतलाच्छतरात्मनः ॥ २३ ॥

आत्मारामस्य Who delights in Self शीतलाच्छतरात्मनः whose mind is calm and pure धीरस्य of the wise man कुत्रापि anywhere जिहासा desire to renounce न not कुत्रचित् anywhere नाशः loss वा or अपि even न not अस्ति is.

23. The wise man who delights in the Self and whose mind is calm and pure, has no[1] desire to renounce anything whatsoever, nor[2] does he feel any loss anywhere.

[1] *No etc.*—One who has still the consciousness of the reality of worldly objects, and sees and feels them as other than the Self, may desire to renounce them; but for one who delights in the Self and the Self alone and has transcended desire itself, renunciation is meaningless.

[2] *Nor etc.*—Though the wise one feels no need to renounce, it does not mean that he holds on to worldly objects. He neither holds on to, nor renounces, anything. He lives like a dry leaf moved by the wind; sometimes like a prince having plenty, sometimes like a beggar denuded of all. In either case, he does not feel any sense of gain or loss.

प्रकृत्या शून्यचित्तस्य कुर्वतोऽस्य यदृच्छया ।
प्राकृतस्येव धीरस्य न मानो.नावमानता ॥ २४ ॥

प्रकृत्या Naturally शून्यचित्तस्य of vacant mind यदृच्छया what comes of itself कुर्वंत: doing अस्य this धीरस्य of the wise one प्राकृतस्य इव like an ordinary man मान: honour न not अवमानता dishonour न not (अस्ति is).

24. Naturally of a vacant[1] mind and doing[2] what comes of itself, the wise one, unlike an ordinary man, is not[3] affected by honour or dishonour.

[1] *Vacant*—Because no modifications arise in his mind.

[2] *Doing etc.*—He acts through the momentum of the effects of those actions that are responsible for his life in this world.

[3] *Not etc.*—Because he does not identify himself with the relative aspects of his being, in reference to which alone the sense of honour or dishonour arises.

कृतं देहेन कर्मेदं न मया शुद्धरूपिणा ।
इति चिन्तानुरोधी यः कुर्वन्नपि करोति न ॥ २५ ॥

इदं This कर्म work देहेन by the body कृतं done शुद्ध-रूपिणा of pure nature मया by me न not (कृतम् done) इति चिन्तानुरोधी conforming to such thoughts यः who (सः he) कुर्वन् acting अपि though न not करोति acts.

25. One who acts in conformity with such thoughts as 'this is done by the body and not by me, the pure Self'—such a one, even though acting, does not act.

अतद्वादीव कुरुते न भवेदपि बालिशः ।
जीवन्मुक्तः सुखी श्रीमान् संसरन्नपि शोभते ॥ २६ ॥

जीवन्मुक्तः One who is liberated even while living

अतद्वादी इव like one who does not say that कुरुते acts अपि even though बालिश: dullard न not भवेत् is (स: he) संसरन् being in the world अपि even सुखी happy श्रीमान् blessed शोभते flourishes.

26. The *jivanmukta* acts like one[1] who does not say that he is acting so; but he is not, therefore, a fool.[2] Even[3] though in the world, he is ever happy and blessed.

[1] *One etc.*—a fool. An ordinary, intelligent man is conscious of the motives and aims of his actions, he can specify them when asked. Not so a fool. A *jivanmukta* also acts without any set purpose or motive.

[2] *Fool*—For though seemingly alike, the fool is *below* the normal level, whereas the *jivanmukta* is *above* it. Extremes often look alike.

[3] *Even etc.*—Even though in the world, he is not of the world—hence his happiness and blessedness. There is no harm in being in the world if one is not attached to it. It is only attachment that binds us and makes us unhappy.

नानाविचारसुश्रान्तो धीरो विश्रान्तिमागतः ।
न कल्पते न जानाति न श्रृणोति न पश्यति ॥ २७ ॥

नानाविचारसुश्रान्त: Tired with diverse reasonings विश्रान्तिम् repose आगत: attained धीर: the wise one न not कल्पते thinks न not जानाति knows न not श्रृणोति hears न not पश्यति sees.

27. The wise one who, weary[1] of diverse reasonings, has attained repose, neither[2] thinks nor knows nor hears nor sees.

¹ *Weary etc.*—in search of Truth, which he found at last as above all reasoning.

² *Neither etc.*—Because he is devoid of the sense of egoism.

असमाघेर्विक्षेपान्न मुमुक्षुर्न चेतरः ।
निश्चित्य कल्पितं पश्यन् ब्रह्मैवास्ते महाशयः ॥ २८ ॥

महाशयः The wise one अविक्षेपात् for having no distraction असमाघेः not practising meditation मुमुक्षुः aspirant for liberation न not इतरः the reverse (i.e. bound) च and न not (भवति is सर्वं all) कल्पितं figment (इति this) निश्चित्य knowing for certain पश्यन् seeing (अपि though सः he) ब्रह्म Brahman एव as आस्ते lives.

28. As the wise one has no distraction and does not practise meditation, he is neither an aspirant for liberation nor is he in bondage. Having known the universe to be a figment even though he sees it, he exists as¹ Brahman Itself.

¹ *As etc.*—untouched by the actions of his mind and senses and unaffected by the universe, that is, in the Absolute state.

यस्यान्तः स्यादहङ्कारो न करोति करोति सः ।
निरहङ्कारधीरेण न किञ्चिद्धि कृतं कृतम् ॥ २९ ॥

यस्य Whose अन्तः within अहंकारः egoism स्यात् is सः he न not करोति acts (अपि though) करोति acts निरहंकार-धीरेण by the wise one who is free from egoism हि surely कृतं done (अपि though) किञ्चित् anything न not कृतम् is done.

29. He who has egoism in him acts[1] even though he does not act.[2] Surely the wise one who is free from egoism does not act even though he acts.

[1] *Acts*—mentally.

[2] *Act*—physically.

Egoism is really the mainspring of all our actions, internal and external. We may refrain from physical actions but not from mental ones, as long as there is egoism in us. It is only with the destruction of the sense of egoism that true inactivity comes. With egoism inaction becomes action, and without egoism action becomes inaction.

नोद्विग्नं न च सन्तुष्टमकर्तृ स्पन्दवर्जितम् ।
निराशं गतसन्देहं चित्तं मुक्तस्य राजते ॥ ३० ॥

मुक्तस्य Of the liberated one चित्तं mind उद्विग्नं troubled न not सन्तुष्टम् pleased च and न not (तथा so also) अकर्तृ स्पन्दवर्जितम् actionless and motionless निराशं desireless गतसन्देहं free from doubts राजते shines.

30. The mind of the liberated one is neither[1] troubled nor[2] pleased; it is actionless,[3] motionless,[4] desireless,[5] and free from doubts.

[1] *Neither etc.*—because of freedom from hatred.

[2] *Nor etc.*—because of freedom from attachment.

[3] *Actionless*—because of freedom from egoism.

[4] *Motionless*—because of freedom from volition.

[5] *Desireless etc.*—Because the liberated one sees no duality, which alone gives rise to desires and doubts.

निध्यातुं चेष्टितुं वापि यच्चित्तं न प्रवर्तते ।
निर्निमित्तमिदं किन्तु निध्यायति विचेष्टते ॥ ३१ ॥

यच्चित्त' Whose mind निध्यातु' to meditate चेष्टितु to act वा अपि or else न not प्रवर्तंते exerts किन्तु but इदं this निर्निमित्तम् without any motive निध्यायति meditates विचेष्टते acts (च and).

31. The mind of the liberated one does not exert itself to be either meditative or active; but it becomes meditative and active without any motive.

The idea is this: The mind of the liberated one is absolutely freed from egoism and consequently from all inclinations and disinclinations which are generated by it. But his body does not drop off immediately after the attainment of Knowledge. His *prārabdha karmas* persist, and his life continues till they are completely exhausted. During this latter period of his life, his actions are entirely guided by his *prārabdha* without the least vestige of egoism or any motive in him. Sometimes he is found active, and sometimes meditative and inactive; internally, however, his condition is always one of absolute freedom and serenity.

तत्त्वं यथार्थमाकर्ण्य मन्दः प्राप्नोति मूढताम् ।

अथवायाति सङ्कोचममूढः कोऽपि मूढवत् ॥ ३२ ॥

मन्दः A dull-witted person यथार्थम् real तत्त्वं truth आकर्ण्य hearing मूढताम् bewilderment प्राप्नोति gets अथवा or कः अपि some अमूढः wise man मूढवत् like a dull person सङ्कोचम् आयाति withdraws within.

32. A dull-witted person becomes bewildered[1] on hearing the real truth, but some[2] sharp-witted man withdraws[3] within himself like a dull person.

[1] *Bewildered etc.*—Because an aspirant for Truth is required to possess certain preliminary qualifications (for

which see Chapter I, verse 1, note 3) in order to qualify
himself even to hear it. Devoid of such qualifications,
he is sure to be bewildered when he hears it. Only those
who have completely purged themselves of all impurities
of mind are fit to hear it and proceed towards its attainment.

² *Some etc.*—It has been repeatedly said in the scriptures that Self-knowledge is very rare in the world. 'One,
perchance, in thousands of men, strives for perfection;
and one, perchance, among the blessed ones striving
thus, knows Me in reality' (*Gītā* VII. 3). The *Kathopa-
niṣad* very clearly brings out the constitutional defect in
man and the consequent rarity of Self-knowledge. It
says: 'The Self-existent God has so created the senses
that they go outward, and hence man sees the external
and not the internal Self. Only, perchance, some wise
man desirous of immortality turns his eyes inwards and
beholds the inner Ātman' (II. 4. 1).

³ *Withdraws etc.*—becomes inactive like a dull person. The dull person, however, is internally quite active,
for all his sense-cravings function; while the wise man,
being without desires, is inactive even internally.

एकाग्रता निरोधो वा मूढैरभ्यस्यते भृशम् ।
धीराः कृत्यं न पश्यन्ति सुप्तवत् स्वपदे स्थिताः ॥ ३३ ॥

मूढैः By the ignorant एकाग्रता concentration निरोध:
control of the mind वा or भृशम् repeatedly अभ्यस्यते is
practised स्वपदे in the real Self स्थिताः abiding धीराः the
wise सुप्तवत् like persons in sleep कृत्यं anything to be done
न not पश्यन्ति see.

33. The ignorant constantly practise[1] concentration and control of the mind. The wise,
abiding in the real Self, like persons in deep sleep,
do[2] not find anything to be done.

¹ *Practise etc.*—Because they see distraction in themselves due to their identification with body and mind.

² *Do etc.*—Because the wise one, even during the
waking state, remains detached from body-consciousness
in the enjoyment of perfect bliss in the Self, in exactly
the same way as, during deep sleep, we lose all consciousness of body and mind and do not find anything to do.

अप्रयत्नात् प्रयत्नाद्वा मूढो नाप्नोति निर्वृतिम् ।

तत्त्वनिश्चयमात्रेण प्राज्ञो भवति निर्वृतः ॥ ३४ ॥

मूढः The ignorant person अप्रयत्नात् from inaction
प्रयत्नात् from action वा or निर्वृतिम् peace न not आप्नोति
attains प्राज्ञः the wise one तत्त्वनिश्चयमात्रेण merely by knowing the Truth निर्वृतः happy भवति becomes.

34. The ignorant person does not attain peace
either by inaction¹ or by action.² The wise one becomes happy merely by knowing the Truth.

¹ *Inaction*—caused by the suppression of all mental
and bodily activity.

² *Action*—impelled by desire.

Suppression of the mind and the performance of
rituals, or other activities impelled by desire, derive from
the consciousness of the Self as separate from the mind
and body. This consciousness is a mere illusion. It is
born of ignorance and is the cause of all misery. Any
activity, physical or mental, rooted in this consciousness
is the very negation of the consciousness of the true
nature of the Self, the realization of which alone results
in infinite bliss and peace.

शुद्धं बुद्धं प्रियं पूर्णं निष्प्रपञ्चं निरामयम् ।

आत्मानं तं न जानन्ति तत्राभ्यासपराः जनाः ॥ ३५ ॥

तत्र In this world अभ्यासपराः devoted to diverse

practices जना: men शुद्ध॑ pure बुद्ध॑ intelligent प्रियं beloved पूर्णं perfect निष्प्रपञ्च॑ beyond the visible universe निरामयम् untainted तं that आत्मानं Self न not जानन्ति know.

35. In this world those who devote themselves to diverse practices do[1] not know the Self, which is pure, intelligent, beloved,[2] perfect, beyond the universe, and free from any taint.

[1] *Do etc.*—Because their practices are rooted in the consciousness of duality, caused by ignorance.

[2] *Beloved*—The Self alone is the object of our love. It is only on account of the Self that our love is directed to the objects of the world. 'None, my dear, ever loved the husband for the husband's sake; it is the Self, for the sake of which the husband is loved.' (*Bṛhadāraṇyaka Upaniṣad* IV.5.6) This applies to all objects of human love.

नाप्नोति कर्मणा मोक्षं विमूढोऽभ्यासरूपिणा ।
धन्यो विज्ञानमात्रेण मुक्तस्तिष्ठत्यविक्रियः ॥ ३६ ॥

विमूढ: An ignorant person अभ्यासरूपिणा in the form of practice (of control of the mind) कर्मणा by action मोक्षं liberation न not आप्नोति attains धन्य: the blessed one विज्ञानमात्रेण by mere knowledge अविक्रिय: immutable मुक्त: liberated तिष्ठति is.

36. The ignorant person does not attain liberation through repeated practice of control of the mind. The blessed one through mere knowledge becomes free and is unaffected by change.

मूढो नाप्नोति तद्ब्रह्म यतो भवितुमिच्छति ।
अनिच्छन्नपि धीरो हि परब्रह्मस्वरूपभाक् ॥ ३७ ॥

यत: As मूढ: the ignorant person ब्रह्म Brahman भवितुम्
to become इच्छति desires (तत: so) तत् That न not आप्नोति
attains धीर: the wise one हि surely अनिच्छन् without desiring अपि even परब्रह्मस्वरूपभाक् who enjoys the nature of the
Supreme Brahman (भवति becomes).

37. The ignorant person does not attain Brahman, for he desires to become It. The wise one
certainly realizes the nature of the Supreme Brahman, even without desiring to do so.

The idea is this: The desire to become Brahman
grows out of a sense of separateness from It. It is a denial
of our true nature. We are always Brahman. Therefore,
as long as this desire remains, the consummation is not
possible. One has to eradicate even the desire for freedom
in order to attain freedom. Freedom has not to be attained.
It is ever attained. We are bound simply because we
think ourselves bound.

निराधारा ग्रह्व्यग्रा मूढा: संसारपोषका: ।
एतस्यानर्थमूलस्य मूलच्छेद: कृतो बुधै: ॥ ३८ ॥

निराधारा: Supportless ग्रह्व्यग्रा: eager for attainment
मूढा: the ignorant संसारपोषका: sustainers of the world
बुधै: by the wise अनर्थमूलस्य the root of misery एतस्य of
this मूलच्छेद: cutting the root कृत: is done.

38. Without[1] any support and eager[2] for the
attainment of freedom, the ignorant[3] only keep up
the world. The wise cut the very root[4] of this world
which is the source of all misery.

[1] *Without etc.*—Self-knowledge is the basis of our
true being. The ignorant do not have it, and hence they
are so called.

[2] *Eager etc.*—through the suppression of the body and mind.

[3] *Ignorant etc.*—by thinking of and behaving with the world as real and so trying to get rid of it. The world is real simply because we think it to be so. When our view of it is changed and we look upon it as non-different from the Self, it ceases to bind us.

[4] *Root etc.*—ignorance.

न शान्तिं लभते मूढो यतः शमितुमिच्छति ।
धीरस्तत्त्वं विनिश्चित्य सर्वदा शान्तमानसः ॥ ३९ ॥

यतः As मूढः the fool शमितुम् to be calm इच्छति desires (ततः so) शान्तिं peace न not लभते attains धीरः the wise one तत्त्वं Truth विनिश्चित्य knowing सर्वदा ever शान्तमानसः of peaceful mind (भवति becomes).

39. The fool[1] desires peace through control of the mind and so does not attain it. The wise one knows the Truth[2] and is ever of a tranquil mind.

[1] *Fool etc.*—We do not find peace simply because we are ignorant of the true nature of the Self, which is calmness itself. Practice of control of the mind is the outcome of ignorance. As long as there is effort for mental control, there must be ignorance, so peace cannot be attained.

[2] *Truth*—his true nature which is tranquillity itself.

कात्मनो दर्शनं तस्य यद्दृष्टमवलम्बते ।
धीरास्तं तं न पश्यन्ति पश्यन्त्यात्मानमव्ययम् ॥ ४० ॥

यद्दृष्टम् (यस्य दृष्टं) Whose knowledge (दृश्यम् object) अवलम्बते depends on तस्य his आत्मनः of the Self दर्शनं knowledge क where धीराः the wise तं तं this and that

न not पश्यन्ति see (किन्तु but) अव्ययम् immutable आत्मानम्
Self पश्यन्ति see.

40. Where is Self-knowledge for him whose
knowledge depends[1] on the object? The wise do[2] not
see this and that but see the immutable Self.

[1] *Depends etc.*—is relative and not absolute, i.e. who
sees duality. Relative knowledge is dependent on three
factors—the knower, the known, and the knowing;
but this triad is lost in Absolute Knowledge.

[2] *Do etc.*—Because they have transcended the relative
consciousness in which the manifold appears.

क निरोधो विमूढस्य यो निर्बन्धं करोति वै ।
स्वारामस्यैव धीरस्य सर्वदाऽसावकृत्रिमः ॥ ४१ ॥

य: Who वै (expletive) निर्बन्धं करोति strives (तस्य
that) विमूढस्य of the deluded one क where निरोध: control of mind स्वारामस्य who delights in the Self धीरस्य
of the wise one असौ that सर्वदा always अकृत्रिम: spontaneous एव surely.

41. Where[1] is control of mind for the deluded
one who strives for it? It[2] is indeed always natural[3]
with the wise one who delights in the Self.

[1] *Where etc.*—Perfect control of mind springs from
complete detachment from body and mind. It therefore
negates all forms of activity which presuppose identification of oneself with them.

[2] *It*—control of mind.

[3] *Natural*—Because calmness is of the very nature of
the Self.

भावस्य भावकः कश्चिन्न किश्चिद्भावकोऽपरः ।
उभयाभावकः कश्चिदेवमेव निराकुलः ॥ ४२ ॥

कश्चित् Someone भावस्य of existence भावकः who
thinks अपरः someone else न किश्चिद्भावकः who thinks that
nothing is कश्चित् एव rarely one उभयाभावकः who thinks
neither एवम् thus निराकुलः free from distraction (अस्ति is).

42. Some think that existence is, and others
that nothing is. Rare[1] is the one who thinks neither
and is thus calm.

[1] *Rare etc.*—He who realizes the Self attains Unity.
No thought whatsoever is possible for him as to the
reality or unreality of the world. He is therefore perfectly
calm and peaceful.

शुद्धमद्वयमात्मानं भावयन्ति कुबुद्धयः ।
न तु जानन्ति संमोहाद्यावज्जीवमनिर्वृताः ॥ ४३ ॥

कुबुद्धयः Men of dull intellect आत्मानं the Self शुद्धम्
pure अद्वयम् without a second भावयन्ति think संमोहात् owing
to delusion तु but न not जानन्ति know (अतः so) यावज्जीवम्
as long as they live अनिर्वृताः unhappy (सन्ति are).

43. Those of dull intellect think that the Ātman
is pure and One without a second, but, through
delusion, they do not know It and are unhappy as
long as they live.

Delusion stands as a bar to Self-realization. Therefore people of dull and deluded intellect do not realize
the true nature of the Self, even though they may hear
and think about It. Their thoughts move within relativity
and cannot transcend it. For them the realization of the
Self, which is Absolute and beyond relative knowledge, is

thus impossible. On the other hand, Self-realization dawns upon those of the purest intellect, which is free from the least tinge of delusion, the moment they hear about the true nature of the Self.

मुमुक्षोर्बुद्धिरालम्बमन्तरेण न विद्यते ।
निरालम्बैव निष्कामा बुद्धिर्मुक्तस्य सर्वदा ॥ ४४ ॥

मुमुक्षो: Of one longing for liberation बुद्धि: intellect आलम्बम् support अन्तरेण without न not विद्यते remains मुक्तस्य of the liberated one बुद्धि: intellect सर्वदा ever निरालम्बा without support निष्कामा free from desire एव surely (विद्यते remains).

44. The intellect of one who longs for liberation cannot[1] function without depending on the object; but the intellect of the liberated one is indeed ever independent and free from desire.

[1] *Cannot etc.*—Because the ignorant person does not realize, as the liberated person does, that the Self is undifferentiated Knowledge, free from the subject-object relationship.

विषयद्वीपिनो वीक्ष्य चकिताः शरणार्थिनः ।
विशन्ति झटिति क्रोडं निरोधैकाग्रसिद्धये ॥ ४५ ॥

विषयद्वीपिन: The tigers of sense-objects वीक्ष्य seeing चकिता: the frightened ones शरणार्थिन: seeking refuge निरोधैकाग्रसिद्धये for attaining control and concentration झटिति at once क्रोडं cave विशन्ति enter.

45. Seeing those tigers the sense-objects, the frightened[1] ones, seeking refuge, at once enter a cave for the attainment of control and concentration.

[1] *Frightened etc.*—The ignorant feel afraid because they look upon sense-objects as different from the Self. The sense of duality is the basic source of fear and misery.

निर्वासनं हरिं दृष्ट्वा तूष्णीं विषयदन्तिनः ।
पलायन्ते न शक्तास्ते सेवन्ते कृतचाटवः ॥ ४६ ॥

निर्वासनं Desireless हरिं lion दृष्ट्वा seeing विषयदन्तिनः the elephants of sense-objects तूष्णीं quietly पलायन्ते run away न not शक्ताः able (सन्तः being) ते they कृतचाटवः flatterers (इव like) सेवन्ते serve.

46. Seeing the desireless lion (man), those elephants, the sense-objects, quietly take to their heels, or, if unable to run away, serve him like flatterers.

The idea in the preceding and the present verses is this: It is not the sense-objects themselves that cause misery, it is one's identification with them, one's attachment for them, that cause misery. Once free from identification and attachment, one need not shun the world. Even in the midst of worldly objects such a one can live freely and happily quite unaffected.

न मुक्तिकारिकां धत्ते निःशङ्को युक्तमानसः ।
पश्यन् शृण्वन् स्पृशन् जिघ्रन्नश्नन्नास्ते यथासुखम् ॥ ४७ ॥

निःशङ्कः Free from doubts युक्तमानसः one whose mind is identified with the Self मुक्तिकारिकां practices of control as a means to liberation न not धत्ते adopts पश्यन् seeing शृण्वन् hearing स्पृशन् touching जिघ्रन् smelling अश्नन् eating (सः he) यथासुखम् happily आस्ते lives.

47. He who is free from doubts and has his mind identified with the Self, does[1] not resort to

practices of control as a means to liberation. Seeing, hearing, touching, smelling, and eating, he lives happily.

[1] *Does etc.*—Because he is free from egoism. Practices of control derive from the sense of duality.

वस्तुश्रवणमात्रेण शुद्धबुद्धिर्निराकुलः ।
नैवाचारमनाचारमौदास्यं वा प्रपश्यति ॥ ४८ ॥

वस्तुश्रवणमात्रेण By the mere hearing of the Real शुद्ध-बुद्धि: who has attained Pure Knowledge निराकुल: calm (ज्ञानी wise one) आचारम् proper conduct अनाचारम् improper conduct औदास्यं indifference वा or न not एव indeed प्रपश्यति sees.

48. Established in Pure Knowledge, and calm by[1] the mere hearing of the Real, the wise one does[2] not see what is proper or improper action or even inaction.

[1] *By etc.*—This is a rare case of Self-realization. No sooner does an aspirant of exceptional merit, whose mind has been completely purified, hear about the nature of the Self, than the Truth dawns upon him.

[2] *Does etc.*—Because he is absolutely free from egoism with the dawn of Self-knowledge, and the rules of conduct have no meaning for him.

यदा यत्कर्तुमायाति तदा तत्कुरुते ऋजुः ।
शुभं वाप्यशुभं वापि तस्य चेष्टा हि बालवत् ॥ ४९ ॥

यदा When यत् which शुभं good वा अपि (expletive) अशुभं evil वा or अपि even कर्तुम् to do आयाति comes तदा then धीर: wise one ऋजु: (सन्) freely तत् that कुरुते does हि

for तस्य his चेष्टा action बालवत् like that of a child (भवति is).

49. The wise one does freely[1] whatever comes to be done, whether[2] good or evil; for his actions are like those of a child.

[1] *Freely*—being free from the sense of egoism.

[2] *Whether etc.*—The wise one is devoid of the idea of 'doer' and purposiveness, which determines one's ethical conduct. His actions therefore transcend all ethical implications.

स्वातन्त्र्यात् सुखमाप्नोति स्वातन्त्र्यादलभते परम् ।

स्वातन्त्र्यान्निर्वृतिं गच्छेत् स्वातन्त्र्यात् परमं पदम् ॥ ५० ॥

(जन: One) स्वातन्त्र्यात् from freedom सुखम् happiness आप्नोति attains स्वातन्त्र्यात् from freedom परम् the highest लभते attains स्वातन्त्र्यात् from freedom निर्वृतिं tranquillity गच्छेत् attains स्वातन्त्र्यात् from freedom परमं Supreme पदम् State (गच्छेत् attains).

50. Through freedom one attains to happiness, through freedom to the highest, through freedom to tranquillity, and through freedom to the Supreme State.

अकर्तृत्वमभोक्तृत्वं स्वात्मनो मन्यते यदा ।

तदा क्षीणा भवन्त्येव समस्ताश्चित्तवृत्तयः ॥ ५१ ॥

यदा When (कश्चित् one) स्वात्मन: of one's own self अकर्तृत्वम् that one is not the doer अभोक्तृत्वं that one is not the enjoyer मन्यते perceives तदा then समस्ता: all चित्तवृत्तय: modifications of the mind क्षीणा: destroyed भवन्ति become.

51. All the modifications of the mind are destroyed when a man realizes that he himself is
neither the doer nor the enjoyer.

उच्छृङ्खलाप्यकृतिका स्थितिर्धीरस्य राजते ।
न तु सस्पृहचित्तस्य शान्तिर्मूढस्य कृत्रिमा ॥ ५२ ॥

धीरस्य Of the wise one अकृतिका inartificial स्थितिः
life उच्छृङ्खला unrestricted अपि though राजते shines सस्पृह-
चित्तस्य whose mind is attached मूढस्य of the deluded person कृत्रिमा feigned शान्तिः calmness तु but न not (राजते
shines).

52. The conduct of the wise one, which is unrestricted by motive, shines, being free from pretence; but not the affected calmness of the deluded
person whose mind is attached.

The idea is this: Generally speaking, when we re-
strain our conduct and appear calm, we do so with a
motive. We want to give the impression that our thought
and feeling correspond with the appearance of our actions.
This is insincerity and pretence and is assumed by one
who is ignorant. It is the pretended calmness of an attached mind. This attitude is the greatest enemy of spiritual
unfoldment, and creates more and more bondages. The
wise one, however, is completely free from attachment.
His actions are absolutely free from egoism and are therefore motiveless. They transcend all limitations.

विलसन्ति महाभोगैर्विशन्ति गिरिगह्वरान् ।
निरस्तकल्पना धीरा अबद्धा मुक्तबुद्धयः ॥ ५३ ॥

निरस्तकल्पना: Who are free from mental projections
अबद्धा: unbound मुक्तबुद्धयः of unfettered intellect धीरा: the

wise (कदाचित् sometimes) महाभोगे: with great enjoyments विलसन्ति sport (कदाचित् sometimes) गिरिगह्वरान्
caves of mountain विशन्ति enter.

53. The wise who are free from mental projections, unbound, and of unfettered[1] intellect, sometimes sport in the midst of great enjoyments, and
sometimes retire into mountain caves.

[1] *Unfettered*—by egoism.

The wise one remains the same and unaffected under
all conditions. He lives, moves, and has his being in the
Self alone, guided only by *prārabdha*.

श्रोत्रियं देवतां तीर्थमज्ञनां भूपतिं प्रियम् ।
दृष्ट्वा सम्पूज्य धीरस्य न कापि हृदि वासना ॥ ५४ ॥

श्रोत्रियं One versed in the Vedas देवतां god तीर्थं
holy place सम्पूज्य honouring अज्ञनां woman भूपतिं king प्रियं
beloved one दृष्ट्वा seeing धीरस्य of the wise one हृदि in the
heart का अपि any वासना desire न not (जायते springs).

54. No[1] desire whatsoever springs in the heart of
the wise one on honouring a man versed in sacred
learning, a god, or a holy place, or on seeing a
woman, a king, or a beloved one.

[1] *No etc.*—Because he sees the Divine essence in
everything and has perfect equanimity.

भृत्यै: पुत्रै: कलत्रैश्च दौहित्रैश्चापि गोत्रजै: ।
विहस्य धिक्कृतो योगी न याति विकृतिं मनाक् ॥ ५५ ॥

भृत्यै: By servants पुत्रै: by sons कलत्रै: by wives च
(expletive) दौहित्रै: by daughter's sons गोत्रजै: by relatives

च and विहस्य ridiculing धिक्कृत: despised अपि though योगी
the *yogin* मनाक् in the least विकृतिं perturbation न not
याति undergoes.

55. The *yogin*[1] is not at all perturbed even when
ridiculed and despised by his servants, sons, wives,
daughter's sons, and other relations.

[1] *Yogin etc.*—Because he is completely free from
delusion which causes attachment and aversion, which,
in turn, perturb the mind.

सन्तुष्टोऽपि न सन्तुष्टः खिन्नोऽपि न च खिद्यते ।
तस्याश्चर्यदशां तां तां तादृशा एव जानते ॥ ५६ ॥

(योगी *Yogin*) सन्तुष्ट: pleased अपि though सन्तुष्ट: pleased न not (भवति is) खिन्न: afflicted अपि though न not खिद्यते
feels distressed च and तस्य his तां तां that and that
आश्चर्यदशां wonderful state तादृशा: those like him एव alone
जानते know.

56. Though[1] pleased he is not pleased, though
pained he does not suffer any pain. Only[2] those
who are like him understand his wonderful state.

[1] *Though etc.*—Pleasure and pain are different modifications of the mind and pertain to it alone. But the Self
is completely unidentified with the mind. The man of
Knowledge, therefore, though outwardly appearing to
feel pleasure and pain, is not at all affected by them.

[2] *Only etc.*—Because his external behaviour is not very
different from that of ordinary people. (Cf. Chapter XIV,
verse 4).

कर्तव्यतैव संसारो न तां पश्यन्ति सूरयः ।
शून्याकारा निराकारा निर्विकारा निरामयाः ॥ ५७ ॥

कर्तंव्यता The sense of duty एव indeed संसार: world of relativity (भवति is) शून्याकारा: of the form of void निराकारा: formless निर्विकारा: immutable निरामया: untainted सूरय: the wise तां that न not पश्यन्ति see.

57. The sense[1] of duty, indeed, is the world of relativity. It is transcended by the wise one who realizes himself as all-pervasive, formless, immutable, and untainted.

[1] *Sense etc.*—It is from the sense of the reality of the world, and from attachment to worldly objects, that the sense of duty arises. This binds us more and more to the world, and thus subjects us to the round of birth and rebirth. (See also verse 3, note 1, of this chapter.)

अकुर्वंन्नपि संक्षोभात् व्यग्र: सर्वंत्र मूढधी: ।
कुर्वंन्नपि तु कृत्यानि कुशलो हि निराकुल: ॥ ५८ ॥

मूढधी: One of dull intellect अकुर्वंन् without doing anything अपि even संक्षोभात् owing to distraction सर्वंत्र at all times व्यग्र: agitated (भवति is) कुशल: the skilful one तु but हि surely कृत्यानि duties कुर्वंन् doing अपि even निराकुल: unperturbed (भवति is).

58. One of dull intellect, even without doing anything, is ever agitated by distraction; but the skilful one, even doing his duties, is verily unperturbed.[1]

[1] *Unperturbed*—Because his mind is ever calm and tranquil, even in the midst of activities, owing to the absence of any egoistic feeling which alone is the source of distraction.

सुखमास्ते सुखं शेते सुखमायाति याति च ।
सुखं वक्ति सुखं भुङ्क्ते व्यवहारेऽपि शान्तधीः ॥ ५९ ॥

व्यवहारे In practical life अपि even शान्तधीः even-
minded (ज्ञानी the wise one) सुखम् happily आस्ते sits सुखं
happily शेते sleeps सुखम् happily आयाति comes याति goes च
and सुखं happily वक्ति speaks सुखं happily भुङ्क्ते eats.

59. With perfect equanimity, even[1] in practical
life, the wise one sits happily, sleeps happily, moves
happily, speaks happily, and eats happily.

[1] *Even etc.*---For the liberated one fictitious differentia-
tion between existence in the Self and existence in the
world completely vanishes. Life becomes one without
bifurcation. He ever lives in the Self alone. Unidentified
with the senses and unattached to sense-objects, he is in
the world but not of the world, merely appearing to perform all the functions of the senses.

स्वभावाद्यस्य नैवार्तिर्लोकवद्व्यवहारिणः ।
महाह्रद इवाक्षोभ्यो गतक्लेशः सुशोभते ॥ ६० ॥

व्यवहारिणः Acting (अपि even) स्वभावात् एव by virtue of the realization of his own self यस्य whose लोकवत्
like ordinary people आर्तिः distress न not (भवति is सः he)
गतक्लेशः with sorrows gone महाह्रदः vast lake इव like
अक्षोभ्यः unagitated सुशोभते shines.

60. Whoever, by virtue of the realization of his
own self, does not feel distressed even in practical
life like ordinary people, and remains unagitated
like a vast lake, with all his sorrows gone—he shines.

निवृत्तिरपि मूढस्य प्रवृत्तिरुपजायते ।
प्रवृत्तिरपि धीरस्य निवृत्तिफलभागिनी ॥ ६१ ॥

मूढस्य Of the deluded one निवृत्ति: inaction अपि even
प्रवृत्ति: action उपजायते becomes धीरस्य of the wise one
प्रवृत्ति: action अपि even निवृत्तिफलभागिनी sharing in the
fruit of inaction (भवति is).

61. With the deluded, even inaction[1] becomes
action; and with the wise, even action[2] results in the
fruit of inaction.

[1] *Inaction etc.*—Because the deluded one, though outwardly inactive, is inwardly most active as his sense of
egoism has not been destroyed.

[2] *Action etc.*—Because the wise one, though he may
be outwardly active, is inwardly completely inactive,
inasmuch as he is not identified with his body and senses
through which all actions are performed.

परिग्रहेषु वैराग्यं प्रायो मूढस्य दृश्यते ।
देहे विगलिताशस्य क रागः क विरागता ॥ ६२ ॥

मूढस्य Of the deluded one परिग्रहेषु in possessions
वैराग्यं aversion प्राय: often दृश्यते is seen देहे in body विगलि-
ताशस्य of one whose attachment has vanished क where
राग: attachment क where विरागता aversion.

62. The deluded[1] one often shows aversion[2] to
his possessions.[3] Where[4] is attachment, where is
aversion for him whose love for the body has vanished?

[1] *Deluded*—who identifies himself with his body and is
therefore attached to it.

² *Aversion*—For the worldly man aversion is occasion-
ed by satiety, as one overfed feels aversion for food. But
this is for the time being, as appetite soon returns.

³ *Possessions*—which are the necessary concomitants
of attachment to the body.

⁴ *Where etc.*—Because both attachment and aversion
are born of the body idea.

भावनाभावनासक्ता दृष्टिर्मूढस्य सर्वदा ।

भाव्यभावनया सा तु स्वस्थस्याद्दृष्टिरूपिणी ॥ ६३ ॥

मूढस्य Of the deluded one दृष्टि: consciousness सर्वदा
always भावनाभावनासक्ता attached to thinking and not-
thinking (भवति is) स्वस्थस्य of one established in the Self
तु but सा that भाव्यभावनया engaged in thinking the thinkable अदृष्टिरूपिणी of the nature of unconsciousness
(भवति is).

63. The consciousness of the deluded one is
always¹ attached to thinking and not-thinking.
But the consciousness of the wise one, though attended with thinking the thinkable, is of² the nature of
unconsciousness.

¹ *Always etc.*—Because he identifies himself with the
mind—the instrument of thinking, and thinks of the
objects of thought as real.

² *Of etc.*—Because the wise one is free from egoism
and knows the objects of thought to be unreal. His consciousness is free from such dualities as things known
and acts of knowing. He is established in Pure Consciousness, the Self.

सर्वारम्भेषु निष्कामो यश्चरेद्बालवन्मुनिः ।

न लेपस्तस्य शुद्धस्य क्रियमाणेऽपि कर्मणि ॥ ६४ ॥

य: मुनि: The wise one who सर्वारम्भेषु in all actions
निष्काम: unattached (सन् being) बालवत् like a child चरति
moves शुद्धस्य pure तस्य of him क्रियमाणे which is being
done कर्मणि to work अपि even लेप: attachment न not
(भवति is).

64. The wise one who has no motive in all his
actions, who moves like a child and is pure, has no
attachment even to the work that is being done by
him.

स एव धन्य आत्मज्ञः सर्वभावेषु यः समः ।
पश्यन् श्रृण्वन् स्पृशन् जिघ्रन्नश्नन्निस्तर्षमानसः ॥ ६५ ॥

स: That आत्मज्ञ: knower of the Self धन्य: blessed एव
indeed य: who निस्तर्षमानस: having transcended the mind
पश्यन् seeing श्रृण्वन् hearing स्पृशन् touching जिघ्रन् smelling
अश्नन् eating (अपि even) सर्वभावेषु in all conditions सम:
same.

65. Blessed indeed is that knower of the Self
who[1] has transcended the mind, and who, even
though seeing, hearing, touching, smelling, or
eating, is the same under all conditions.

[1] *Who etc.*—literally, whose mind is free from thirst
and craving.

क संसारः क चाभासः क साध्यं क च साधनम् ।
आकाशस्येव धीरस्य निर्विकल्पस्य सर्वदा ॥ ६६ ॥

आकाशस्य इव Like the firmament सर्वदा ever निर्वि-
कल्पस्य changeless धीरस्य of the wise one क where संसार:

world क where च (expletive) आभास: appearance क
where साध्यं end क where च and साधनम् means.

66. Where is the world and where its appearance, where is the end[1] and where the means,[2] for
the wise one who is ever changeless like the firmament?

[1] *End*—liberation.
[2] *Means*—spiritual practices.

The man of Knowledge sees nothing but himself
outside and inside. To him nothing but the Self exists.
He has therefore nothing to attain and consequently no
occasion for spiritual practices, the means to Self-realization.

स जयत्यर्थसंन्यासी पूर्णस्वरसविग्रहः ।
अकृत्रिमोऽनवच्छिन्ने समाधिर्यस्य वर्तते ॥ ६७ ॥

यस्य Whose अनवच्छिन्ने in the unconditioned अकृत्रिमः
spontaneous समाधिः absorption वर्तते is सः that अर्थसंन्यासी
free from all desires पूर्णस्वरसविग्रहः who is the perfect
embodiment of bliss which is his own nature जयति is
glorious.

67. Glorious is he who is free from all desires,
who is the perfect embodiment of bliss which is his
own nature, and who is spontaneously absorbed in
the unconditioned Self.

बहुनात्र किमुक्तेन ज्ञाततत्त्वो महाशयः ।
भोगमोक्षनिराकांक्षी सदा सर्वत्र नीरसः ॥ ६८ ॥

अत्र Here बहुना much उक्तेन by saying किम् what
need ज्ञाततत्त्व: who has known the Truth महाशय: the

great-souled one भोगमोक्षनिराकांक्षी free from the desire of enjoyment and liberation सदा at all times सर्वत्र in all places नीरस: devoid of attachment (भवति is).

68. In short, the great-souled one who has realized the Truth is free from the desire for enjoyment and liberation and is devoid of all attachment at all times and in all places.

महदादि जगद्‌द्वैतं नाममात्रविजृम्भितम् ।
विहाय शुद्धबोधस्य किं कृत्यमवशिष्यते ॥ ६९ ॥

नाममात्रविजृम्भितम् Manifested through mere name महदादि beginning with *mahat* जगद्‌द्वैतं the phenomenal existence विहाय renouncing शुद्धबोधस्य of one who is Pure Consciousness कृत्यम् to be done किं what अवशिष्यते remains.

69. What remains to be done by one who is Pure Consciousness? He has renounced phenomenal[1] existence which begins with *mahat* and is manifested[2] through mere name.

[1] *Phenomenal etc.*—According to the Sāṃkhya philosophy, *Prakṛti* (the undifferentiated) is the primal cause of this universe. Out of *Prakṛti* evolves *mahat* (cosmic intelligence) from which *ahaṃkāra* (egoism) proceeds, and from that again mind, the five organs of the senses, the five organs of action, and the five *tanmātras* (fine elements) arise. The five *tanmātras* produce five *mahābhūtas* (gross elements) which make up this gross material universe.

[2] *Manifested etc.*—As such, the phenomenal universe is unreal and illusory. It is superimposed through ignorance on the Self which is the indivisible, infinite One, and is the basis of all apparent manifoldness.

The wise one ever remains unidentified with the world and free from the false consciousness of duties.

भ्रमभूतमिदं सर्वं किञ्चिन्नास्तीति निश्चयी ।
अलक्ष्यस्फुरणः शुद्धः स्वभावेनैव शाम्यति ॥ ७० ॥

इदं This सर्वं all भ्रमभूतम् produced from illusion किञ्चित् anything न not अस्ति exists इति this निश्चयी knowing for certain अलक्ष्यस्फुरणः to whom the imperceptible is revealed शुद्धः the pure one स्वभावेन by nature एव indeed शाम्यति enjoys peace.

70. The pure[1] one knows for certain that this universe is the product of illusion and that nothing exists. The Imperceptible[2] Self is revealed to him, and he naturally[3] enjoys peace.

[1] *Pure*—free from ignorance.

[2] *Imperceptible etc.*—The Self is beyond the mind and the senses. It cannot be objectified. Nothing can perceive It; but It is self-luminous. Though unknowable, It is known to itself by itself.

[3] *Naturally*—Because bliss and peace are the very essence of his true nature.

शुद्धस्फुरणरूपस्य दृश्यभावमपश्यतः ।
क विधिः क च वैराग्यं क त्यागः क शमोऽपि वा ॥ ७१ ॥

शुद्धस्फुरणरूपस्य Of the nature of Pure Effulgence दृश्यभावम् the objective reality अपश्यतः not seeing (जनस्य of one) विधिः rule of conduct क where वैराग्यं dispassion च and क where त्यागः renunciation क where शमः restraint of the senses अपि also वा or क where.

71. Rule of conduct, dispassion, renunciation, and restraint of the senses—what are all these to one who is of the nature of Pure Effulgence and who does not perceive any objective reality?

स्फुरतोऽनन्तरूपेण प्रकृतिं च न पश्यतः ।
क बन्धः क च वा मोक्षः क हर्षः क विषादिता ॥ ७२ ॥

अनन्तरूपेण As the Infinite स्फुरतः shining प्रकृतिं relative existence च and न not पश्यतः seeing (जनस्य of one) क where बन्धः bondage कृ where च and मोक्षः liberation कृ where हर्षः joy कृ where वा or विषादिता sorrow.

72. Where is bondage or liberation, joy or sorrow for one who shines as the Infinite and does not perceive relative existence?

बुद्धिपर्यन्तसंसारे मायामात्रं विवर्तते ।
निर्ममो निरहङ्कारो निष्कामः शोभते बुधः ॥ ७३ ॥

बुद्धिपर्यन्तसंसारे In the world existing until Self-knowledge मायामात्रं mere illusion विवर्तते prevails बुधः the wise one निर्ममः devoid of 'mine-ness' निरहङ्कारः devoid of 'I-ness' निष्कामः free from attachment शोभते excels.

73. Only the illusion of the world prevails. The reality of the world vanishes with the knowledge of the Self. The wise one lives without the feeling of 'I-ness' and 'mine-ness', and attachment.

अक्षयं गतसन्तापमात्मानं पश्यतो मुनेः ।
क विद्या च क वा विश्वं क देहोऽहं ममेति वा ॥ ७४ ॥

अक्षयं Imperishable गतसन्तापम् free from grief आत्मानं Self पश्यत: seeing मुने: of the wise one क where विद्या knowledge कृ where च and विश्व universe कृ where वा or अहं देह: I am the body मम (देह:) the body is mine वा or इति (expletive).

74. To the wise one who perceives the Self as imperishable and free from grief, where is knowledge and where is the universe? Where is the feeling 'I am the body' or 'the body is mine'?

निरोधादीनि कर्माणि जहाति जडधीर्यदि ।
मनोरथान् प्रलापांश्च कर्तुमाप्नोत्यतत्क्षणात् ॥ ७५ ॥

यदि If जडधी: one of dull intellect निरोधादीनि control etc. कर्माणि practices जहाति gives up (तर्हिं then) अतत्क्षणात् from that very moment मनोरथान् desires प्रलापान् fancies च and कर्तुं to do आप्नोति begins.

75. No sooner does the man of dull intellect give up such practices as mind-control than he becomes a prey to desires and fancies.

It has been said repeatedly that the man of Self-knowledge is completely devoid of dual consciousness caused by ignorance and, consequently, of all efforts to control the senses. The idea expressed here is that for the ignorant person also, persisting as he does in the dual vision, practices of control are of little avail, since as soon as there is a lapse in his practices, he is dragged down to the mire of desires.

The implication is that Self-knowledge is not a thing to be attained by practices of control. It already is and has to be realized as such.

मन्दः श्रुत्वापि तद्वस्तु न जहाति विमूढताम् ।
निर्विकल्पो बहिर्यत्नादन्तर्विषयलालसः ॥ ७६ ॥

मन्दः The dull one तत् that वस्तु Reality श्रुत्वा hearing
अपि even विमूढताम् delusion न not जहाति gives up यत्नात्
through effort बहिः externally निर्विकल्पः with mental
actions suppressed (अपि though) अन्तः internally विषय-
लालसः craving for sense-objects (भवति is).

76. Even hearing the Truth, the man[1] of dull
intellect does not give up his delusion. Though,[2]
through suppression, he appears devoid of mental
activity, a craving for sense-objects lurks within
him.

[1] *Man etc.*—Because delusion vanishes only with
Self-knowledge.

[2] *Though etc.*—Because one can get rid of desire only
through Self-knowledge and not by suppression.

ज्ञानाद्गलितकर्मा यो लोकदृष्ट्यापि कर्मकृत् ।
नाप्नोत्यवसरं कर्तुं वक्तुमेव न किञ्चन ॥ ७७ ॥

यः Who ज्ञानात् owing to Knowledge गलितकर्मा whose
work has dropped (सः he) लोकदृष्ट्या in the sight of
the people कर्मकृत् doing work अपि even किञ्चन anything कर्तुं to do न not वक्तुम् to say एव even न not अवसरं
opportunity आप्नोति gets.

77. He whose work has ceased with the dawn of
Knowledge does not find an opportunity to do or
say anything, even though in ordinary people's
eyes he is doing work.

The idea is that true inaction is not the cessation of physical activity, but the doer's freedom from the conceit of 'I am the doer'.

क तमः क प्रकाशो वा हानं क च न किञ्चन ।
निर्विकारस्य धीरस्य निरातङ्कस्य सर्वदा ॥ ७८ ॥

सर्वदा Ever निर्विकारस्य immutable निरातङ्कस्य fearless धीरस्य of the wise one कृ where तमः darkness कृ where वा or प्रकाशः light कृ where हानं loss किञ्चन anything च and न not (भवति is).

78. For the wise one who is ever immutable and fearless, where[1] is there darkness, where light? Where, moreover, is there any loss? There is nothing whatsoever.

[1] *Where etc.*—Darkness, light, and other sensuous objects are possible only in the domain of duality, but not where there is but One, the unchanging Self.

क धैर्यं क विवेकित्वं क निरातङ्कतापि वा ।
अनिर्वाच्यस्वभावस्य निःस्वभावस्य योगिनः ॥ ७९ ॥

अनिर्वाच्यस्वभावस्य Of indescribable nature निःस्वभावस्य impersonal योगिनः of the *yogin* कृ where धैर्यं patience क where विवेकित्वं discrimination कृ where निरातङ्कता fearlessness अपि even वा or.

79. Where is patience, where is discrimination, and where, even, is fearlessness for the *yogin* who is impersonal and of indescribable nature?

न स्वर्गो नैव नरको जीवन्मुक्तिर्न चैव हि ।
बहुनात्र किमुक्तेन योगदृष्ट्या न किञ्चन ॥ ८० ॥

स्वर्गं: Heaven न not नरक: hell एव also न not जीव-
न्मुक्ति: liberation while alive एव even च and न not हि
surely अत्र here किम् what need बहुना much उक्तेन by saying योगदृष्ट्या in *yogic* vision किञ्चन anything न not
(विद्यते exists).

80. There is no heaven, and there is no hell;
there is not even liberation-in-life. In short, nothing[1]
exists in *yogic* consciousness.

[1] *Nothing*—nothing but the Self.

नैव प्रार्थयते लाभं नालाभेनानुशोचति ।
धीरस्य शीतलं चित्तममृतेनैव पूरितम् ॥ ८१ ॥

(स: He) लाभं gain न not प्रार्थयते longs for एव
surely अलाभेन at non-attainment न not अनुशोचति grieves
धीरस्य of the wise one शीतलं cool चित्तम् mind अमृतेन with
nectar एव verily पूरितम् filled.

81. The wise one neither longs for gain nor
grieves at non-attainment. His cool mind is verily
filled with nectar.[1]

[1] *Nectar*—of Supreme Bliss.

न शान्तं स्तौति निष्कामो न दुष्टमपि निन्दति ।
समदुःखसुखस्तृप्तः किञ्चित् कृत्यं न पश्यति ॥ ८२ ॥

निष्काम: One who is free from desire शान्तं one
who is calm न not स्तौति praises दुष्टम् one who is wicked
अपि even न not निन्दति blames तृप्त: contented समदुःखसुख:
same in happiness and misery (स: he) कृत्यं to be done
किञ्चित् anything न not पश्यति sees.

82. The desireless one neither praises the calm nor blames even the wicked. Contented and the same in happiness and misery, he finds nothing to be done.

धीरो न द्वेष्टि संसारमात्मानं न दिदृक्षति ।
हर्षामर्षविनिर्मुक्तो न मृतो न च जीवति ॥ ८३ ॥

धीर: The wise one संसारम् the round of birth and rebirth न not द्वेष्टि hates आत्मानं the Self न not दिदृक्षति wishes to perceive हर्षामर्षविनिर्मुक्त: free from joy and sorrow (स: he) न not मृत: dead न not जीवति lives च and.

83. This wise one neither[1] abhors birth and rebirth nor wishes to perceive the Self. Free from joy and sorrow, he is neither[2] dead nor alive.

[1] *Neither etc.*—The need for liberation is consequent upon the idea of metempsychosis. Being the Self already, the wise one has neither metempsychosis nor liberation. Therefore he neither shrinks from the one nor craves the other.

[2] *Neither etc.*—Life and death imply change. The Self being changeless and eternal, the man of Self-knowledge has neither.

निःस्नेह: पुत्रदारादौ निष्कामो विषयेषु च ।
निश्चिन्तः स्वशरीरेऽपि निराशः शोभते बुधः ॥ ८४ ॥

पुत्रदारादौ In son, wife, and others निःस्नेह: free from attachment विषयेषु in sense-objects च and निष्काम: free from desire स्वशरीरे for his own body अपि even निश्चिन्त:

free from care निराश: free from expectation बुध: the wise
one शोभते lives in glory.

84. Glorious is the life of the wise one, free
from expectation, free from attachment for children,
wife, and others, free from desire for the objects of
the senses, and free from the care of even his own
body.

तुष्टि: सर्वत्र धीरस्य यथापतिततवर्तिनः ।
स्वच्छन्दं चरतो देशान्यत्रास्तमितशायिनः ॥ ८५ ॥

यथापतितवर्तिन: Who lives on whatever happens to
come to him देशान् countries स्वच्छन्दं at pleasure चरत:
wandering यत्रास्तमितशायिन: resting wherever the sun sets
धीरस्य of the wise one सर्वत्र everywhere तुष्टि: contentment
(भवति is).

85. Contentment ever dwells in the heart of
the wise one who lives on whatever happens to come
to him, and who wanders about at pleasure, resting
wherever he is when the sun sets.

पततूदेतु वा देहो नास्य चिन्ता महात्मनः ।
स्वभावभूमिविश्रान्तिविस्मृताशेषसंसृते: ॥ ८६ ॥

देह: The body पततु may drop down उदेतु may rise
वा or अस्य this स्वभावभूमिविश्रान्तिविस्मृताशेषसंसृते: who has
completely transcended birth and rebirth owing to his
repose on the foundation of his own being महात्मन: of the
great-souled one ।चन्ता care न not (भवति is).

86. Reposing[1] on the foundation of his own

being, and completely transcending birth and rebirth, the great-souled one does not care whether
his body dies or is born.

[1] *Reposing etc.*—The body, mind, and the entire world
are superimposed on the Self. Changes in them, therefore, do not affect the man of Self-knowledge.

अकिञ्चनः कामचारो निर्द्वन्द्वश्छिन्नसंशयः ।
असक्तः सर्वभावेषु केवलो रमते बुधः ॥ ८७ ॥

अकिञ्चनः Without any possession कामचारः moving
at pleasure निर्द्वन्द्वः free from the pairs of opposites छिन्न-
संशयः whose doubts have been rent asunder सर्वभावेषु in
all things असक्तः unattached केवलः alone बुधः the wise one
रमते rejoices.

87. Blessed is the wise one who stands alone,[1]
who is attached to nothing, who is without[2] any
possession, who moves freely and at pleasure, who
is free from the pairs of opposites, and whose doubts
have been rent asunder.

[1] *Alone*—aloof, as witness.
[2] *Without etc.*—The Self being One without a second,
the man of Knowledge has nothing else to possess.

निर्ममः शोभते धीरः समलोष्टाश्मकाञ्चनः ।
सुभिन्नहृदयग्रन्थिर्विनिर्धूतरजस्तमः ॥ ८८ ॥

निर्ममः Devoid of the feeling of 'mine' समलोष्टाश्म-
काञ्चनः to whom earth, stone or gold is the same
सुभिन्नहृदयग्रन्थिः the knots of whose heart have been completely severed विनिर्धूतरजस्तमः who has been purged
of *rajas* and *tamas* धीरः the wise one शोभते excels.

88. Glorious is the wise one who is devoid of the feeling of 'mine', to whom earth, a stone, and gold are all the same, the knots of whose heart have been rent asunder, and who has been purged[1] of *rajas* and *tamas*.

[1] *Purged etc.*—*Sattva*, *rajas*, and *tamas* are the three constituents of *Prakṛti*. The whole of internal and external nature is composed of them. *Sattva* is the principle of knowledge and delight. *Rajas* is the principle of motivity and pain. *Tamas* is the principle of inertia and ignorance. When *rajas* and *tamas* prevail in the mind, it cannot perceive the true nature of the Self. *Sattva* alone can reflect the self-effulgent Ātman. So the mind must be purged of *rajas* and *tamas* before the glory of Ātman may manifest.

सर्वत्रानवधानस्य न किञ्चिद्वासना हृदि ।
मुक्तात्मनो वितृप्तस्य तुलना केन जायते ॥ ८९ ॥

(यस्य Whose) हृदि in the heart किञ्चित् any वासना desire न not (अस्ति is तस्य that) सर्वत्रानवधानस्य indifferent to all objects वितृप्तस्य contented मुक्तात्मनः of the liberated soul केन with whom तुलना comparison जायते is.

89. Who is there to stand comparison with the liberated soul who has no desire whatsoever at heart, who is contented and indifferent to everything?

जानन्नपि न जानाति पश्यन्नपि न पश्यति ।
ब्रुवन्नपि न च ब्रूते कोऽन्यो निर्वासनादृते ॥ ९० ॥

निर्वासनात् ऋते Except the desireless one अन्यः other कः who जानन् knowing अपि even न not जानाति knows

पश्यन् seeing अपि even न not पश्यति sees ब्रुवन् speaking
अपि even न not ब्रूते speaks च and.

90. Who but the desireless one knows not
though knowing, sees not though seeing, and speaks
not though speaking?

भिक्षुर्वा भूपतिर्वापि यो निष्कामः स शोभते ।
भावेषु गलिता यस्य शोभनाशोभना मतिः ॥ ९१ ॥

यस्य Whose भावेषु at things शोभनाशोभना good and
evil मतिः view गलिता dropped यः who निष्कामः unattached
सः he भिक्षुः mendicant वा (expletive) भूपतिः king वा or
अपि (expletive) शोभते excels.

91. Be he a mendicant or a king, he excels who
is unattached and whose[1] view of things has been
freed from the sense of good and evil.

[1] *Whose etc.*—Because he finds nothing but the Self
existing in all, good and evil.

क स्वाच्छन्द्यं क सङ्कोचः क वा तत्त्वविनिश्चयः ।
निर्व्याजार्जवभूतस्य चरितार्थस्य योगिनः ॥ ९२ ॥

निर्व्याजार्जवभूतस्य Who is the embodiment of guileless sincerity चरितार्थस्य who has attained his desired end
योगिनः of the *yogin* स्वाच्छन्द्यं wantonness क where सङ्कोचः
restraint कु where तत्त्वविनिश्चयः determination of Truth
वा or कु where.

92. Where[1] is wantonness, where is restraint,
and where[2] is determination of Truth for the *yogin*
whose life's object has been fulfilled and who is the
embodiment of guileless sincerity?

¹ *Where etc.*—The idea of 'doer' and purposiveness determines one's ethical conduct. Being established in the Self, the One without a second, the *yogin* is devoid of both. His actions, therefore, transcend all ethical implications.

² *Where etc.*—Determination of Truth loses its relevance when Truth stands self-revealed as one's Ātman.

आत्मविश्रान्तितृप्तेन निराशेन गतार्तिना ।

अन्तर्यदनुभूयेत तत्कथं कस्य कथ्यते ॥ ६३ ॥

आत्मविश्रान्तितृप्तेन Who is contented with repose in the Self निराशेन desireless गतार्तिना whose sorrow is over (जनेन by one) अन्त: within यत् which अनुभूयेत is experienced तत् that कथं how कस्य to whom कथ्यते can be said.

93. How¹ and to whom can be described what is experienced within by one who is desireless, whose sorrow is destroyed, and who is contented with repose in the Self ?

¹ *How etc.*—Because the Self is beyond mind and speech.

सुप्तोऽपि न सुषुप्तौ च स्वप्नेऽपि शयितो न च ।

जागरेऽपि न जागर्ति धीरस्तृप्तः पदे पदे ॥ ६४ ॥

सुषुप्तौ In sound sleep अपि even न not सुप्त: asleep च (expletive) स्वप्ने in dream अपि even च and न not शयित: lying जागरे in waking state अपि even न not जागर्ति is awake धीर: the wise one पदे पदे under all conditions तृप्त: contented.

94. Not[1] asleep, even when sleeping soundly; not lying down, even when dreaming; and not awake, even in the waking state; such is the wise one who is contented under all conditions.

[1] *Not etc.*—Sleep, dreaming, and wakefulness, the three states of mind, are illumined by the changeless Self which stands as the eternal Witness. He who has become established in the Self, therefore, remains unaffected by these states of mind.

ज्ञः सचिन्तोऽपि निश्चिन्तः सेन्द्रियोऽपि निरिन्द्रियः ।
सुबुद्धिरपि निर्बुद्धिः साहङ्कारोऽनहंकृतिः ॥ ९५ ॥

ज्ञः The man of Knowledge सचिन्तः engaged in thought अपि though निश्चिन्तः devoid of thought सेन्द्रियः possessed of the organs of sense अपि though निरिन्द्रियः devoid of the organs of sense सुबुद्धिः possessed of intelligence अपि though निर्बुद्धिः devoid of intelligence साहङ्कारः possessed of egoism (अपि though) अनहंकृतिः devoid of egoism.

95. The man of Knowledge is devoid of thought, even when he is engaged in thought; he is devoid of the sense-organs, even though he has them; he is devoid of intelligence, even though endowed with it; and he is devoid of the sense of ego, even though possessed of it.

Dwelling ever in the transcendence of Pure Consciousness, the man of Self-knowledge is *ipso facto* unidentified with the mind and the senses, though he may appear to behave like an ordinary man.

न सुखी न च वा दुःखी न विरक्तो न सङ्गवान् ।
न मुमुक्षुर्न वा मुक्तो न किश्चिन्न च किश्चन ॥ ९६ ॥

(ज्ञः The wise one) सुखी happy न not दुःखी miserable च and न not विरक्तः unattached न not सङ्गवान् attached वा or न not मुमुक्षुः aspirant for liberation न not मुक्तः liberated वा or न not किञ्चित् something न not किञ्चन anything च and न not.

96. The man of Knowledge is neither[1] happy nor miserable, neither attached nor unattached, neither liberated nor an aspirant for liberation; he is neither this nor that.

[1] *Neither etc.*—Happiness, misery, liberation, bondage, and other such attributes can never be predicated of the Self which is One, indescribable, and eternally free.

विक्षेपेऽपि न विक्षिप्तः समाधौ न समाधिमान् ।
जाड्येऽपि न जडो धन्यः पाण्डित्येऽपि न पण्डितः ॥ ९७ ॥

धन्यः The blessed one विक्षेपे in distraction अपि even विक्षिप्तः distracted न not समाधौ in meditation (अपि even) समाधिमान् meditative न not जाड्ये in dullness अपि even जडः dull न not पाण्डित्ये in learning अपि even पण्डितः learned न not.

97. The blessed one is not distracted even in distraction; he is not meditative even in meditation; he is not dull even in a state of dullness; and he is not learned even though possessed of learning.

The man of Knowledge is other than what he appears to be. He realizes the Self as distinct from his body and mind, and stands aloof as Pure Consciousness. He is unconcerned with all mental operations, not to speak of the physical.

मुक्को यथास्थितिस्वस्थः कृतकर्तव्यनिवृतः ।
समः सर्वत्र वैतृष्ण्यान्न स्मरत्यकृतं कृतम् ॥ ९८ ॥

यथास्थितिस्वस्थः Abiding in the Self in all conditions
कृतकर्तव्यनिवृतः free from the idea of action and of duty
सर्वत्र everywhere समः same मुक्तः liberated one वैतृष्ण्यात्
owing to desirelessness अकृतं what has not been done
कृतम् what has been done न not स्मरति reflects upon.

98. The liberated one who abides in the Self
under all conditions, who is free from the idea of
action and of duty, and who is the same everywhere,
does[1] not, owing to desirelessness, reflect upon what
he has or has not done.

   [1] *Does etc.*—The ego and its offspring, desire, precede
all sense of action and duty. Being completely free from
them, the liberated soul remains ever unconcerned with
all his actions, past, present, and future.

न प्रीयते वन्द्यमानो निन्द्यमानो न कुप्यति ।
नैवोद्विजति मरणे जीवने नाभिनन्दति ॥ ९९ ॥

(ज्ञानी The wise one) वन्द्यमानः praised न not प्रीयते
is pleased निन्द्यमानः blamed न not कुप्यति is annoyed
जीवने in life न not अभिनन्दति rejoices मरणे at death न
not उद्विजति fears एव surely.

   99. Praised,[1] the wise one does not feel pleased;
and blamed, he does not feel annoyed. He neither
rejoices in life, nor fears death.

   [1] *Praised etc.*—Being ever identified with the Absolute
Self, One without a second, there can be for him no
praiser and no praise, no blamer and no blame; and
neither life nor death.

न धावति जनाकीर्णं नारण्यमुपशान्तधीः ।

यथातथा यत्रतत्र सम एवावतिष्ठते ॥ १०० ॥

उपशान्तधीः The man whose mind is calm जनाकीर्णं crowded place न not धावति runs after अरण्यम् forest (अपि even) न not (धावति runs after सः he) यथातथा in any way यत्रतत्र anywhere समः same एव verily अवतिष्ठते lives.

100. The tranquil-minded one seeks neither the crowded place nor the wilderness. He remains the same[1] under any conditions and in any place.

[1] *Same etc.*—being established in Self-knowledge and enjoying the infinite bliss of his own nature.

CHAPTER XIX

REPOSE IN THE SELF

जनक उवाच ।

तत्त्वविज्ञानसन्दंशमादाय हृदयोदरात् ।
नानाविधपरामर्शशल्योद्धारः कृतो मया ॥ १ ॥

जनकः Janaka उवाच said:

मया By me तत्त्वविज्ञानसन्दंशम् the pincers of the knowledge of Truth आदाय taking हृदयोदरात् from the inmost recesses of my heart नानाविधपरामर्शशल्योद्धारः the extraction of the thorn of the different judgements कृतः is done.

Janaka said:

1. I have extracted from the inmost recesses of my heart the thorn[1] of different opinions, using the pincers of the knowledge of Truth.

Janaka, the disciple, having heard about the bliss of the Self and realized it, now recounts in the following eight verses, for the satisfaction of his Guru, his own repose in the Self.

[1] *Thorn etc.*—Doubts and varying opinions are always a great obstacle to the vision of Truth, causing extreme anguish to the aspiring soul. Just as a thorn is extracted by means of a pair of pincers, so the thorn of doubts and varying opinions can be removed by the light of Knowledge transmitted by a true seer.

क धर्मः क च वा कामः क चार्थः क विवेकिता ।
क द्वैतं क च वाऽद्वैतं स्वमहिम्नि स्थितस्य मे ॥ २ ॥

स्वमहिम्नि In my own glory स्थितस्य abiding मे my
धर्मः meritorious works कृ where कामः sense enjoyment च
and कृ where अर्थः prosperity च and कृ where विवेकिता
discrimination वा or कृ where द्वैतं duality कृ where अद्वैतं
non-duality च and कृ where वा (expletive).

2. Where is *dharma*, where is *kāma*, where is
artha? Where, too, is discrimination, where is
duality, and where, even, is non-duality for me who
abide in my own glory?

क भूतं क भविष्यद्वा वर्तमानमपि क वा ।
क देशः क च वा नित्यं स्वमहिम्नि स्थितस्य मे ॥ ३ ॥

स्वमहिम्नि स्थितस्य मे For me abiding in my own glory
भूतं past कृ where भविष्यत् future वा or कृ where वर्तमानम्
present अपि even वा or कृ where देशः space वा or कृ
where नित्यं eternity च and कृ where.

3. Where is the past; where is the future, where,
even, is the present? Where is space, and where,
even, is eternity for me who abide in my own glory?

क चात्मा क च वानात्मा क शुभं काशुभं तथा ।
क चिन्ता क च वाचिन्ता स्वमहिम्नि स्थितस्य मे ॥ ४ ॥

स्वमहिम्नि स्थितस्य मे For me abiding in my own glory
आत्मा Self च (expletive) कृ where अनात्मा not-Self च and
कृ where शुभं good कृ where तथा as also अशुभं evil कृ where

14

चिन्ता anxiety वा or कृ where अचिन्ता non-anxiety च and कृ where वा (expletive).

4. Where is the Self and where is the non-Self, where, likewise, are good and evil, where is anxiety or non-anxiety for me who abide in my own glory?

क स्वप्नः क सुषुप्तिर्वा क च जागरणं तथा ।
क तुरीयं भयं वापि स्वमहिम्नि स्थितस्य मे ॥ ५ ॥

स्वमहिम्नि स्थितस्य मे For me abiding in my own glory स्वप्नः dream कृ where सुषुप्तिः deep sleep वा or कृ where तथा as also जागरणं wakefulness कृ where तुरीयं fourth (state) च and कृ where भयं fear अपि even वा or (कृ where).

5. Where is dreaming, where is deep sleep, where is wakefulness, and where is the fourth[1] state; where, even, is fear for me who abide in my own glory?

[1] *Fourth etc.*—The word *turīya* literally means fourth. So long as ignorance prevails, the Self is conditioned by three states—wakefulness, dreaming, and deep sleep. With the dawn of Knowledge it attains the fourth state of transcendental bliss. This is said to be the fourth only with reference to the three previous states, otherwise the Absolute is beyond any relational determination.

क दूरं क समीपं वा बाह्यं काभ्यन्तरं क वा ।
क स्थूलं क च वा सूक्ष्मं स्वमहिम्नि स्थितस्य मे ॥ ६ ॥

स्वमहिम्नि स्थितस्य मे For me who abide in my own glory दूरं distance कृ where समीपं near वा or कृ where

बाह्य exterior क् where अभ्यन्तरं interior वा or क् where स्थूलं gross क् where सूक्ष्मं subtle वा or क् where च (expletive).

6. Where is distance, where is proximity; where is exterior, where is interior; where is grossness, and where is subtlety for me who abide in my own glory?

क मृत्युर्जीवितं वा क लोकाः कास्य क लौकिकम् ।
क लयः क समाधिर्वा स्वमहिम्नि स्थितस्य मे ॥ ७ ॥

स्वमहिम्नि स्थितस्य मे For me who abide in my own glory जीवितं life क् where मृत्युः death वा or क् where अस्य (मम) my लोकाः worlds क् where लौकिकम् worldly relation क् where लयः lapse क् where समाधिः concentration वा or क् where.

7. Where is life or death, where are the worlds, and where are worldly relations; where is lapse,[1] and where is concentration for me who abide in my own glory?

[1] *Lapse—Laya* is the lapse of the mind into sleep without resting on the Absolute. It is one of the four obstacles to *samādhi*, the other three being *vikṣepa* (distraction), *kaṣāya* (torpidity), and *rasāsvāda* (enjoyment of *savikalpa samādhi*).

अलं त्रिवर्गकथया योगस्य कथयाप्यलम् ।
अलं विज्ञानकथया विश्रान्तस्य ममात्मनि ॥ ८ ॥

आत्मनि In Self विश्रान्तस्य reposing मम my त्रिवर्गकथया of talking about the three ends of life अलं needless

योगस्य of *yoga* कथया of talking अलम् needless विज्ञानकथया of talking about wisdom अपि even अलं needless.

8. To talk about the three ends of life is needless, to talk about *yoga* is purposeless, and even to talk about wisdom is irrelevant for me who repose in the Self.

CHAPTER XX

LIBERATION-IN-LIFE

जनक उवाच ।

क भूतानि क देहो वा केन्द्रियाणि क वा मनः ।
क शून्यं क च नैराश्यं मत्स्वरूपे निरञ्जने ॥ १ ॥

जनकः Janaka उवाच said:

निरञ्जने Taintless मत्स्वरूपे in myself भूतानि elements
क्व where देहः body वा or क्व where इन्द्रियाणि organs क्व
where मनः mind वा or क्व where शून्यं void क्व where
नैराश्यं despair च and क्व where.

Janaka said:

1. Where are the elements, where is the body,
where are the organs, and where is the mind; where
is the void; where, too, is despair for me who am
taintless by nature?

The disciple now describes the state of a free soul
which, even while in life, follows upon repose in the
Self.

क शास्त्रं कात्मविज्ञानं क वा निर्विषयं मनः ।
क तृप्तिः क वितृष्णत्वं गतद्वन्द्वस्य मे सदा ॥ २ ॥

सदा Ever गतद्वन्द्वस्य devoid of the sense of duality
मे for me शास्त्रं scripture क्व where आत्मविज्ञानं Self-
knowledge क्व where निर्विषयं not attached to sense-objects

मन: mind वा or कृ where तृप्ति: contentment कृ where
वितृष्णत्वं desirelessness कृ where.

2. Where are the scriptures, where is knowledge of the Self, where is the mind not attached to
sense-objects, where is contentment, and where is
desirelessness for me who am ever devoid of the
sense of duality?

क विद्या क च वाविद्या काहं केदं मम क वा ।

क बन्धः क च वा मोक्षः स्वरूपस्य क रूपिता ॥ ३ ॥

विद्या Knowledge कृ where अविद्या ignorance च and
कृ where अहं 'I' कृ where इदं 'this' वा or कृ where मम
'mine' वा or कृ where बन्ध: bondage कृ where मोक्ष:
liberation वा or कृ where (मम) स्वरूपस्य of the nature
of my self रूपिता attribute च and कृ where.

3. Where is Knowledge and where is ignorance;
where is 'I', where is 'this', and where is 'mine';
where is bondage and where is liberation? Where
is an attribute to the nature of my self ?

क प्रारब्धानि कर्माणि जीवन्मुक्तिरपि क वा ।

क तद्विदेहकैवल्यं निर्विशेषस्य सर्वदा ॥ ४ ॥

सर्वदा Ever निर्विशेषस्य undifferentiated (मे for me)
प्रारब्धानि commenced कर्माणि actions कृ where जीवन्मुक्ति:
liberation-in-life अपि even कृ where तत् that विदेहकैवल्यं
liberation-at-death वा or कृ where.

4. Where are *prārabdha karmas*, where[1] is liberation-in-life, and where is even liberation-at-death
for me, the ever undifferentiated?

¹ *Where etc.*—To a man of Self-knowledge liberation-in-life is a contradiction and is as much a creation of ignorance as bondage. He denies life itself; and he denies liberation altogether. Liberation presupposes bondage, but the Self is ever existent, ever unborn, ever free; It has never been born; It has never been in bondage. The idea even of liberation is consequently a serious limitation to the seeker of wisdom, for it screens him from the true nature of the Self.

The same truth applies to liberation-at-death, in which state the Self is permanently dissociated from the body. But the idea of such emancipation also presupposes the truth of body and of bondage, and therefore goes directly against the true nature of the Self. (Cf. Ch. XVIII, verse 13, notes, and verse 18, note 1).

क कर्ता क च वा भोक्ता निष्क्रियं स्फुरणं क वा ।
क्वापरोक्षं फलं वा क निःस्वभावस्य मे सदा ॥ ५ ॥

सदा Ever निःस्वभावस्य impersonal मे for me कर्ता doer क where भोक्ता enjoyer वा or च (expletive) क where निष्क्रियं cessation of activity (thinking) स्फुरणं rising of thought वा or क where अपरोक्षं direct knowledge क where फलं reflected knowledge वा or क where.

5. Where is the doer or the enjoyer, where is cessation of thought or the rising of thought, where is direct knowledge or reflected¹ knowledge, for me who am ever impersonal?

¹ *Reflected etc.*—Each cognition involves two factors —one is the mental modification in the form of the object and the other is the revelation of the object by consciousness reflected on that mental modification. The latter is called *phala*, reflected knowledge. This process applies only in the case of relative knowledge and not in

the case of one who ever dwells in Transcendental Consciousness.

क लोकः क मुमुक्षुर्वा क योगी ज्ञानवान् क वा ।
क बद्धः क च वा मुक्तः स्वस्वरूपेऽहमद्वये ॥ ६ ॥

अहमद्वये स्वस्वरूपे For me who am non-dual in nature लोकः world कृ where मुमुक्षुः aspirant for liberation वा or कृ where योगी the contemplative man कृ where ज्ञानवान् man of Knowledge वा or कृ where बद्धः the soul in bondage कृ where मुक्तः the liberated soul वा or च (expletive) कृ where.

6. Where is the world and where is the aspirant for liberation; where is the contemplative man and where is the man of Knowledge; where is the soul in bondage and where is the liberated soul for me who am non-dual by nature?

क सृष्टिः क च संहारः क साध्यं क च साधनम् ।
क साधकः क सिद्धिर्वा स्वस्वरूपेऽहमद्वये ॥ ७ ॥

अहमद्वये स्वस्वरूपे For me who am non-dual in nature सृष्टिः creation कृ where संहारः destruction च and कृ where साध्यं end कृ where साधनम् means च and कृ where साधकः seeker कृ where सिद्धिः success वा or कृ where.

7. Where are creation and destruction; where is the end and where the means; where are seeker and success for me abiding in my non-dual nature?

क प्रमाता प्रमाणं वा क प्रमेयं क च प्रमा ।
क किञ्चित् क न किञ्चिद्वा सर्वदा विमलस्य मे ॥ ८ ॥

सर्वदा Ever विमलस्य pure मे for me प्रमाता knower क्व
where प्रमाणं the means to knowledge वा or (क्व where)
प्रमेयं the object of knowledge क्व where प्रमा knowledge
च and क्व where किञ्चित् something क्व where न किञ्चित्
nothing वा or क्व where.

8. Where is the knower, the means to knowledge, the object of knowledge, or knowledge itself; where is anything, and where is nothing for
me who am ever pure?

क विक्षेपः क चैकाग्रं क निर्बोधः क मूढता ।
क हर्षः क विषादो वा सर्वदा निष्क्रियस्य मे ॥ ६ ॥

सर्वदा Ever निष्क्रियस्य actionless मे for me विक्षेपः distraction क्व where ऐकाग्र्यं concentration च and क्व where
निर्बोधः full knowledge क्व where मूढता delusion क्व where
हर्षः joy क्व where विषादः sorrow वा or क्व where.

9. Where is distraction, where is concentration;
where is knowledge,[1] where is delusion; where is
joy and where is sorrow for me who am ever actionless?

[1] *Knowledge*—*Nirbodhah* usually means dullness. But
here the contrast is between two opposites. Hence in the
present context *nirbodhah* (*niḥśeṣeṇa bodhaḥ*) means full
knowledge and keeps up the symmetry.

क चैष व्यवहारो वा क च सा परमार्थता ।
क सुखं क च वा दुःखं निर्विमर्शस्य मे सदा ॥ १० ॥

सदा Ever निर्विमर्शस्य devoid of discursive thought
मे for me एषः this व्यवहारः relativity च (expletive) क्व

where सा that परमार्थता transcendence वा or च (expletive) क़ where सुखं happiness क़ where दुःखं misery वा or च (expletive) क़ where.

10. Where is relativity, where is transcendence; where is happiness or misery for me who am ever beyond any discursive thought?

क माया क च संसारः क प्रीतिर्विरतिः क वा ।
क जीवः क च तद्ब्रह्म सर्वदा विमलस्य मे ॥ ११ ॥

सर्वदा Ever विमलस्य pure मे for me माया illusion क़ where संसारः world च and क़ where प्रीतिः attachment क़ where विरतिः detachment वा or क़ where जीवः jīva क़ where तत् that ब्रह्म Brahman च and क़ where.

11. Where is illusion, where is the world; where is attachment or detachment; where is jīva or Brahman for me, who am ever pure?

क प्रवृत्तिर्निवृत्तिर्वा क मुक्तिः क च बन्धनम् ।
कूटस्थनिर्विभागस्य स्वस्थस्य मम सर्वदा ॥ १२ ॥

सर्वदा Ever कूटस्थनिर्विभागस्य immutable and indivisible स्वस्थस्य established in the Self मम for me प्रवृत्तिः activity निवृत्तिः inactivity वा or क़ where मुक्तिः liberation क़ where बन्धनम् bondage च and क़ where.

12. Where is activity, where is inactivity; where is liberation or bondage for me who am ever immutable[1] and indivisible, and established in the Self?

[1] Immutable—kūta means 'a heap', and kūtastha means 'remaining like a heap'; hence, immutable and eternal.

क्वोपदेशः क वा शास्त्रं क शिष्यः क च वा गुरुः ।
क चास्ति पुरुषार्थो वा निरुपाधेः शिवस्य मे ॥ १३ ॥

निरुपाधेः Free from limitation शिवस्य absolute good
मे for me उपदेशः: instruction कृ where शास्त्रं scripture वा
or कृ where शिष्यः: disciple कृ where गुरुः: preceptor वा or
च (expletive) कृ where पुरुषार्थः: object of life वा or च
and कृ where अस्ति is.

13. Where are instruction and scriptural in-
junction, where is the disciple and where is the
preceptor; where, indeed, is the object of life for
me who am absolute good and free from limitation?

क चास्ति क च वा नास्ति कास्ति चैकं क च द्वयम् ।
बहुनात्र किमुक्तेन किञ्चिन्नोत्तिष्ठते मम ॥ १४ ॥

अस्ति Existing च (expletive) कृ where न अस्ति not
existing वा or च (expletive) कृ where एकं unity च (expletive) कृ where अस्ति is द्वयम् duality च and कृ where
(अस्ति is) अत्र here बहुना much उक्तेन by saying किम्
what need मम from me किञ्चित् anything न not
उत्तिष्ठते emanates.

14. Where is existence, where is non-existence;
where is unity, where is duality? What need is there
to say more? Nothing emanates from me.

Aṣṭāvakra concludes his teaching in this verse and
presents his philosophy in a nutshell. He accepts the
reality of the Self alone. There is no world. Nothing
exists besides the Self. There is no appearance even, for
appearance is brought about by ignorance; and the
negation of appearance can only take place in ignorance.

Yet Aṣṭāvakra does not recognize ignorance either, for the assertion of ignorance implies the existence of something other than the Self. He does not recognize either bondage or liberation. Thought creates bondage, and liberation is consequent on the thought of bondage. But true knowledge transcends this cobweb of thought. In truth there is neither bondage nor liberation: these are only states of mind. The Self is ever free, unaffected by any state of mind.

Thus, according to Aṣṭāvakra, there is but One Reality, the infinite, indivisible Self which is Knowledge Absolute, Bliss Absolute. The realization of the Self is the only *summum bonum* and in this alone does life find its fulfilment.

INDEX

ASTAVAKRA SAMHITA

INDEX TO SLOKAS